I want you to see Me

GARY L. RICHARDSON
&
TOM WESTBROOK

with **DAVID WILLETS**

I want you to see Me
© 2017 by Gary L. Richardson & Tom Westbrook

Published by Insight International, Inc.
contact@freshword.com
www.freshword.com
918-493-1718

All rights reserved. No part of this book may be reproduced or transmitted in any form or by any means, electronic or mechanical, including photocopying and recording, or by an information storage and retrieval system, without permission in writing from the author.

Unless otherwise noted all Scripture quotations are taken from *The Holy Bible, New International Version®*, NIV® Copyright © 1973, 1978, 1984, 2011 by Biblica, Inc.® Used by permission. All rights reserved worldwide.

Scripture quotations marked THE MESSAGE are from *The Message*. Copyright © 1993, 1994, 1995, 1996, 2000, 2001, 2002. Used by permission of NavPress Publishing Group.

Scripture quotation marked NET is taken from the NET Bible® copyright ©1996-2016 by Biblical Studies Press, L.L.C. Scripture quoted by permission. All rights reserved.

Scripture quotation marked GNT is taken from the Good News Translation® (*Today's English Version*, Second Edition). Copyright © 1992 American Bible Society. All rights reserved.

Cover design by Jill Westbrook.
Cover Photography by Travis Warren.

ISBN: 978-1-943361-18-2
E-Book ISBN: 978-1-943361-19-9

Library of Congress Control Number: 2016952711

Printed in the United States of America.

CONTENTS

Foreword...5

Acknowledgements...9

Introduction..11

Section 1:
God reveals Himself, and some people's learning curves.

1   Begin Where God Began...17

2   People Who Knew: Traveling Way Beyond Religion.............29

3   Two-faced...43

Section 2:
Our stories: How God reveals His Truth in our lives.

4   My Two-faced Life...63

5   Our Monolith: God...89

6   God's Desert(s) and Finishing School.......................101

7   Finish and Leave the "Lab" of this Desert Experience..........129

Section 3:
What difference does it make?

8   Living in Sovereignty While Here on Earth.......................141

9   The Lord is Willing...161

FOREWORD

Gary, Tom and David — the three authors of *I want you to see Me* — asked if I might write a foreword for this book. I immediately said yes because these men are friends, who know how to enjoy life, embrace truth, and empower others. I know them as fun conversationalists — unafraid to challenge the status quo of religiosity.

However, after reading *I want you to see Me*, I found an even more important reason for writing this foreword. I want to convince you of the great profit coming your way from digesting this book. Notice, I didn't say reading this book, I said "digesting."

I don't like the phrase "self-help" because nobody is ultimately helped apart from God. This book will enable you to see God for who He really is. That is the precise prescription for real change in your life. It's why you must digest the book — "Taste and see that the Lord is good."

When you really see God for who He is, you'll never be the same. The prophet Isaiah "saw the Lord, high and lifted up," and from that moment forward, he was transformed for the better.

God is the "Me" in *I want you to see Me*.

One failing of Old Covenant Israel was their inability to see God. In Psalm 50:21 God said to Israel, "You thought I was exactly like you." We often struggle with the same thing. We think God is like us. We don't see Him the way He really is, the way He reveals Himself to be in His Word.

I want you to see Me

I write this after a rash of mass shootings in America and abroad. Fear grips so many people. *The New York Herald's* headline blares, "God Can't Fix This." Their article expresses a sentiment that God has nothing to do with our world. To *the Herald's* editors, God is distant, impotent, and unimportant.

They don't see God as He really is.

God tells us in Jeremiah 32:27 (NET): "I am the Lord, the God of all humankind. There is, indeed, nothing too difficult for Me." Have you seen this God?

Jesus had about a dozen disciples travel with Him. A fisherman named Phillip was one of Jesus' original followers. One day, some sophisticated Greeks came to Philip asking: "Sir, we would like to see Jesus." Philip immediately took them to see Jesus.

Phillip's seeking Greeks became seeing Greeks: seeing the One in whom "all the fullness of the Godhead bodily dwelt" (Colossians 2:9). Their lives were transformed. Why? Philip knew people must see God as He is, not as they make Him out to be.

Gary, Tom and David are collectively a modern day Philip. They will take you to a place where you will see Jesus in every area of your existence. You'll learn there is no reason to compartmentalize your life between secular and religious, or spiritual and physical, or temporal and eternal. You'll see God in every moment, every event — both good and "bad" — and every hour of life is all of your life that you have, and God is in the middle of it all.

One line in the book summarizes the truth of God's essence so vividly. "In God's geography, deserts aren't 'on the way' or 'in the way.' Deserts, wildness, wilderness, solitude are His ways to achieve great things in people He loves and uses." Do you see God's beauty in every part and parcel of your life?

You and I usually read a book because something drives us to read it. Is it the cover? Or perhaps the title? In my case, I usually pick up a book because it is recommended to me.

FOREWORD

This foreword is my recommendation to read *I want you to see Me*. I want you to see God in everything. I want you to see His goodness, His mercy, His kindness, His wisdom, His power, His providence, His sovereignty, and every other great and mighty attribute He possesses in everything you experience.

Joni Eareckson Tada says, "God will allow those things He hates in order to bring about those things He loves." When you really see your God, you will join in and say what she says about your God.

Gary, Tom and David will take you on a journey to see God. Walk with them as they open up their own lives to help you see God in their experiences. Digest the truth of who God really is as you read. Begin to see God in your life as well. I mean — you will really see Him.

I want you to see Me is to your soul what steak is to your body. When you finish chewing on the nuggets of truth about God that the authors set before you, and when you digest the truth of who God really is, you'll find strength and power in your life you never dreamed of having.

The Scriptures tell us that those who see and know their God will display strength and take action. (Daniel 11:32).

May God give you the grace necessary to see Him in these pages. Maybe, by the very act of picking up this book and reading this far, God is gently and lovingly saying to you, "I want you to see Me!"

—Wade Burleson

Wade is a pastor, writer and avocational historian. He is the pastor of Emmanuel Baptist Church in Enid, Oklahoma.

ACKNOWLEDGEMENTS

My deepest thanks...

My Dad, W. R. (Bill) Richardson. Dad gave me such a security in his love that I could never rest until I knew my Heavenly Father's security for us all. Searching for God's security for me brought me to God's sovereignty.

Lanna, you are God's most precious lady to me. You have blessed me with your kindness, patience, and encouragement to devote the time for this project. Thanks for making the late nights on the computer bearable and always being supportive.

Tom and Jill Westbrook. What talent. Jill did the cover. It's so beautiful. Thank you, Jill.

David Willets. You are a consistent friend and mentor in God's sovereignty.

Bob Baxter. God used my dear friend of over twenty years to bring Tom and me together. You were my sounding board and Devil's Advocate as I wrote.

Wade Burleson. What a giant when it comes to the subject of sovereignty. Thanks, Wade, for the conversations and the confirmations. Thanks for the foreword.

My Monday morning 7 a.m. study group. You guys are special. I have treasured our thirteen years together on Mondays. You have been a great sounding board for me.

I want you to see Me

Everyone: family members, friends, and enemies, who God used to do His work in me. The love, blessings, lessons, or challenges God brought to me through you are everything to me.

INTRODUCTION

(Gary)

We had been working for months on this book and particularly processing some of its more demanding passages when I got to bed late. I dreamed. I awoke and began studying my dream, and in analyzing it the word *yielding* leapt out at me.

In my dream *yielding* was personified. As a force, *it* came to tell me, came to say essentially the same thing four times before this book's message could come forth. As I yielded, parts of this book's message could become clear to me.

So I studied the dream to discover *yielding* came to tell me I'm in a process: "It's a long process of yielding your all, Gary, to the Father. Little is accomplished if God isn't in it." Odd. *Yielding* continued: "I'm here with you. I direct you. I guide as you continue walking in faith. Know I am here. Know that I lead, I guide and I direct you."

Next, I sensed that in *yielding* I will never fear. "Never fear. I'm all you've ever needed. And today, I love you as a son, a son of whom I'm so proud and who I plan to use in a beautiful way."

Third, I knew from *yielding* — Jesus is all true yielding. His nature forms the core of anything any of us know of yielding. He said, "You've been through much, but see my suffering on the cross?

I want you to see Me

I did it for you, for all your brothers, and all your sisters. The Father asked it. How could I not do so?"

I know the Bible has over four hundred names for Jesus,[1] so although new, it was not difficult for me to see Jesus as *Yielding*.

Thanks be to God. This book contains men and women of faith yielding to God their all. It also holds portions of my story giving my all to *Yielding* and His Father.

Last *Yielding*, or Jesus in my dream, pointed out to me, "Your path lies before not behind you. Let yesterday go, to focus on tomorrow. Great is the battle, but greater is the reward. As I teach you a complete surrender — surrendered to Father — you'll find the joy and peace for which you've hungered all your days. Walk the steps My Father has for you."

"Time is not God's issue, only yours. Be patient; calm. Be a Job. Wait on the Lord your God to bring you through . . . and I will."

And then *Yielding*, Jesus, morphed again to say, "Love, your Heavenly Father."

(Tom)

When Gary said he was ready to write this book, I had no idea how much it would push me to wrestle with my own pilgrimage in Christ. I came to two stark moments over the years of writing.

Stark moment number one: We steal a lot here from others. Sir Isaac Newton, himself a believer, was asked how he could form groundbreaking math and physics. Humbly he said, "I stand on the shoulders of giants who went before me!" He stood on their shoulders as Cambridge closed due to the Black Death: God's purpose to Isaac according to his journals.

---

[1] Messiah, First Born from among the Dead, Daystar, Captain, Alpha and Omega are but a few.

INTRODUCTION

One set of shoulders on which we stand belongs to Job, a guy in the Bible, who God used to prove a point to Satan — some men are unshakable. Here is my point. Please, remember this as you read.

Tragedy overwhelmed Job. Three friends came to grieve with him. One brought a young man along making four. At first they walked through Job's low point in life sensitively, poignantly. Barely recognizing Job, they ripped their clothes, threw ashes on their heads and wept with him. Then they sat for seven days in silence, saying nothing. Good. Great friends.

Finally, Job croaked his frustration at God, unflinchingly revealing the depth of his pain and how clueless he was about why God did this. He unleashed a torrent.

Each buddy and even the young guy began to club Job with judgments and theology. Make no mistake. Their theology was wise. It defended God deftly.

Only God wasn't asking anyone to defend Him.

As Job's buddies wielded their theology it became evident — they were using all of it in the wrong place. With the wrong guy. At the wrong time. So they were totally out of line with what God was doing.

So humbly, let us make a request. Don't *ever* use anything in this book without first praying to ask God how it *might* apply to a situation in yours or in someone else's life.

Misplaced theology is a terrible club we can use on each other to great wounding. Job's story is God's flashing yellow light shouting, "Warning! Religion and theology fail you here!" Humbly take all pet answers back to Him and get on His schedule for revealing what He is doing, where He is working in any situation, pain, or trauma.

Return to Job's friends' first acts. Shut up. Listen. Listen again, with tears if they come. Tears with someone are more eloquent than words.

I want you to see Me

I don't know when God will reveal what He is doing. Often, I know He acts and leaves His motivations and outcomes shrouded in mystery until I'm ready to know why He is doing what He is doing, or how He will use it. That can take years.

So don't add this book to your pet answers or formulas. Discard those formulas to daily seek God and listen to what He says, what He shows, what He reveals.

Stark moment number two: David, Gary and I sat in Gary's office, dark wood, deep green, and a couple of bronze eagles that scream larger than life. In the day's cold, gray light on our warm chairs, Gary told part of his life — a possibly frightening diagnosis of cancer. And in the waiting God was whispering to Gary, "Don't see cancer or anything else. I want you to see Me in this."

The book snapped into focus for the first time, all parts of a whole. Sovereign God continually, unerringly says to us all,

"I want you to see Me!"

So we write this book, much like Paul wrote to his friends:

I was unsure of how to go about this, and felt totally inadequate—I was scared to death, if you want the truth of it—and so nothing I said could have impressed you or anyone else. But the Message came through anyway. God's Spirit and God's power did it, which made it clear that your life of faith is a response to God's power, not to some fancy mental or emotional footwork by me or anyone else.[2]

---

[2] 1 Corinthians 2:35, THE MESSAGE.

SECTION 1

God reveals Himself, and some people's learning curves.

1

Begin Where God Began

You must start with love. And end with love.
Start anywhere else, and you don't get God,
or goodness, or hope, or anything.
And if you are not aiming to end with "Truth in Love,"
you will end somewhere else, less. All else is less.

What if we held a contest to find two Bible[3] verses that most shout out God's love to us who believe Christ as Lord? Can you see a long list of candidates? People would nominate so many verses!

Of course, millions would nominate John 3:16: *For God so loved the world that He gave His only Son, that any of us who believe in Him will be saved.* But we would expect hundreds of other verses to flood us, verses bearing God's promises to us in trouble, anxiety, facing death, or promising joy!

Out of all of those verses, we focus on two. These two prove sure to us. Living out that these are true we will never be the same. These two shout out God's goodness to us.

Romans 8:28 We know that in all things God works for the good of those who love Him, who have been called according to His purpose.

---

[3] Looking at the New Testament: the parts of the Bible written after Jesus.

17

I want you to see Me

Philippians 1:6 Being confident of this very thing, that He who began a good work in you will carry it on to completion until the day of Christ Jesus.

We love these verses for so many reasons.

That first verse from Paul to the Church in Rome shouts that God works, using all that happens in our lives for our good. That God will turn *anything* that happens to us who love Him to our good. *Anything* is a long, long list of possible things. The Philippian verse strengthens that great news. It says God is already working in us, and He will carry on His good work to complete us in the day of Christ Jesus.

His work began before we were born into the world, carried through our infancy and childhood and accelerated whenever we professed Christ as Lord.

As bad things happen in our world, as situations around us spiral out of control, as people and situations wound or insult us — we have these breathtaking verses. God is working for our good, using everything that happens to us from now until the end of time.[4]

Again, God works for our good, using all that happens to us from now to the end of time.

You might write that on a piece of paper. Put it on your mirror as a reminder. God is at work for our good, using everything that happens to us from now to the end of time.

See what is and is not in those verses. It clearly says, "For those that love Him, who have been called according to His purpose." It promises this wonder to His children, not to people who neither care about Christ nor live in His purpose. The second verse from Philippians adds nothing on our parts, but the verse in front of it says "we are partners in this work."[5]

---

[4] A host of verses also show God's greatness and love throughout tough times. Two passages are Isaiah 9:6-7 and Isaiah 45:57.

[5] Philippians 1:5.

Well a huge divide has arisen out of the ocean of truth like a continent on our roles "as partners" in what God is doing in us. On one shore of the continent a group says that what God will do, is doing, and can do hinges on whether we are living like "we love Him and have been called according to His purpose." Essentially they assert that as we live like we love God and follow His purpose in us, God responds.

We can't keep our end of the bargain.

Can we love God on our own?

On the other shore, the other group asserts that God initiated this salvation or relationship. God completes this. God empowers this, and He does so as we fail, as we thrash about helplessly, or as we succeed. God is doing what God does, irrespective of whether we keep our end of the bargain. Why?

So, as surely as God always does what He says He will do — we can't keep our end of the bargain. If we could, Jesus would not have needed to come and die for our failures in the first place.

Very good people, very distinguished scholars live and die on both sides of this divide.

We will take a small Bible tour to show why we live on the side that we live, and invite you to live there as well.

First, we start with our relationship with God. Specifically, how does God view our relationship with Him?

Let's go back in time. Christians, Jews and Muslims all see God start a *relationship* with a man named Abram. God chose Abram to finish what his father began, leaving a Babylon neighborhood to go to a land God showed him to claim as a promise. Abram journeyed and had adventures, but the time came for God to make good on

I want you to see Me

part of the promise — millions of heirs — God's promise for Abram. Abe didn't have one heir at age 99!

God tells Abe to fetch a heifer, goat, ram, pigeon and dove.[6] In Abe's day if two people ratified an important contract, they cut the big animals in two, put the two halves opposite each other, and walked through the bloody ground in between the halves. It became sacred ground because of the shed blood. Then they usually ate all the meat in a feast. The story takes a turn here.

Abe slaughters and cuts the big animals in halves. He places the halves opposite each other to make sacred ground, and then God went silent. Abram shooed off vultures until sunset when he dropped into a deep sleep, and God added a deep and dreadful darkness.[7] In a dream, God appears as "a smoking firepot with a blazing torch and passes between the pieces. On that day the Lord made a covenant with Abram."[8]

Abram wakes up and it is done! God made the covenant with Abram.

What was missing? Abram. Abram slaughtered and arranged the animals, but God does not ask Abram to walk between the halves with God. God does not make Abram make a promise. Why?

Abram can't keep his end of a promise. Abram can't keep his end of a relationship. We won't list all Abram's failings, but he tries to manipulate getting an heir and makes a mess. He lies about whether his wife is his wife or "his sister" if other kings look at her longingly! In short, Abram is a failer. He has great faith in God, but he fails at being good. God knew so God made His pact with Abram — alone. All is done from God's side. God does not expect Abram to carry through with his part, so God leaves him snoozing and passes through for both of them!

---

[6]   Genesis 15:9ff.

[7]   Genesis 15:12.

[8]   Genesis 15:17, 18.

Begin Where God Began

God invented the *relationship* in the Bible without our promise, without our ante, on His strength alone! This theme plays throughout the Bible. God works at and builds the possibility of a relationship with Him. We say thanks and fail. Often. Hugely. Amazingly. We fail. In fact as we point to people as saints and amazing people, God whispers that their best acts of being good are like filthy rags to Him.[9]

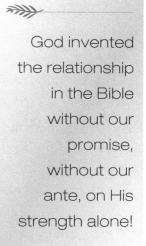

> God invented the relationship in the Bible without our promise, without our ante, on His strength alone!

Now, take what we see in God opening a relationship with Abram and look at the cross of Jesus, again. Scholars tell us that God made covenants with Adam, Noah, Abraham (God changed his name later), Moses, David and finally Jesus. Search that bloody ground on Skull Hill where they crucified Jesus. Do you find anyone from humanity's side on that Cross? Jesus. Fully man. Do you find anyone from God's side on the Cross? Jesus. Fully God. How did Jesus get down here and onto that cross?

God sent Jesus, part of Himself! God initiated! God empowered Jesus to live a perfect life. God raised Jesus from the dead! God carried through. God took Jesus back to heaven. What do any of us do from our side? What do we do to make the pact or open the covenant? We believe; we put our faith in Christ *after* the fact. None of us live perfect lives or die to get anything started. "It" — the entire salvation or *relationship* — does not depend on us.

It's all on God. It's all about what God does. It's all about God. So, we come down on the shore where "It all rests with God." God initiates and God promises. God empowers and God forgives. God calls us, and calls us again. We fail. We welsh on promises. God is consistent.

---

[9] Isaiah 64:6.

I want you to see Me

It's all on God. It's all about what He does. It's all about God. We can't earn anything, unless you think hell is something worth earning. So, why is this important?

It is important because it makes a universe of a difference in how we live; a universe of differences in how we enjoy our trip through life on our way Home.

So many people go to church guilt ridden and sit through mass or church and do penance or try to go out and live and fail and feel terrible. Over and over. Week in and week out. We hear that we are sinners and feel futile, helpless.

So many people go to church to pray and feel as if their prayers don't make it to the ceiling. They aren't worthy of God listening and answering.

So many people preach and teach as if it all depends on us and when we then go out and fail, we think God failed.

So many people try to be good and are failers. (Not failures, just failers.) What a horror story. Let's look at those two verses again.

Romans 8:28 We know that in all things God works for the good of those who love Him, who have been called according to His purpose.

Philippians 1:6 Being confident of this, that He who began a good work in you will carry it on to completion until the day of Christ Jesus.

You believe in Christ because God wants you to believe. You are trying to follow Christ because God began that good work in you. He chose to begin that work in you, and so to finish it. You can trust that God is working in your circumstances for your good, to perfect you, to complete you because He promised. He carries through on His promise to us, even as we fail because He knew we would fail every time we failed.

That is more wonderful than anything else we can imagine. What peace comes with that! What power comes with God's promise!

We come down on the "It's all about God" shore for another reason — and it is big. Unless God holds all of time, all of the possible outcomes, all of the choices of everyone in account with His purposes, God will not deliver on His promises in those two verses that we love so much.

If we believe a mad man, some disease, a historical cataclysm, or trauma can thwart God's promises to us, then we have put our trust in a poor place! In his letter to the Corinthians[10] Paul examines this problem. If God has not resurrected Christ (and us) then this is all a sham. If God didn't deliver on Promise #1 by raising Christ from the dead, it is all religious hocus pocus. Keep your money. Protect your family from this lie. . .

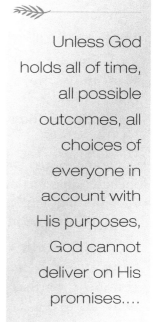

> Unless God holds all of time, all possible outcomes, all choices of everyone in account with His purposes, God cannot deliver on His promises....

If God can't make good on His promise(s), then we of all people are hopeless.

But God's word is true. Christ did die. He is resurrected. When He begins His new work in us, we have this new life in Christ. We have placed our hope in a secure place! We hold on to this amazing hope irrespective of all the mistakes the Church has made, is making daily in the news, and will make. We have this hope in spite of Christians and their failings and conniving and politicking.

It is not about the Church. It is not about Christians. It is about God.

---

[10] 1 Corinthians 15:12-36.

I want you to see Me

We have this hope because it's all on God — where He wants it — where He knew it would work. It's all about what God does: to His glory. It's all about God.

There is a word for whether God can pull it all off. We use this word to describe His ability to make it all work for our good, or complete us as He promised. The word is sovereign. Is God *sovereign*? Can He do all He has promised? Any hope for peace hinges on this.

Some other words also translate that word: sovereign. They include: supreme, dominant, ascendant, predominant, absolute, superior, outstanding, excellent, matchless, peerless, monarch, ruler, and king. All of those fit in the category for sovereign labeled supreme.

Those words define God's (actually they barely scratch the surface) unmatched place in our universe. But here again, that continent that has arisen in the ocean of truth pushing one set of believers to one side and us to the other is important.

We *do* use the word sovereign to describe God as supreme. Check. We *also* use the word sovereign to define whether *we* or some group are independent: autonomous, free, and self-determining.

Hmm. The word sovereign has two domains. Supreme (Who is on top?) and autonomous (Who is free?). Those two domains have fueled a lot of history, especially in the West. With the rise of democracy in the West over the past centuries, what ideas have been attacked most? Granted, in the last few years, we see attacks on the traditional family, the United States' founding values, the middle class, any sense of privacy, and the worth of the individual. Think further.

The trends

What about the last say — eight centuries? We see two trends. One started with *The Magna Carta*.[11] In *The Magna Carta*, English

---

[11] June 15, 1215 was the signing, but it didn't become official law until 1225.

nobles tugged some of the king's rights from him. Ever since, the attack or erosion of monarchs' sovereignty assailed every king or queen on a throne. The United States jump started a process of obliterating kingly sovereignty with our Revolutionary War (Civil War in England!). England slowly implemented many ideas that first saw the light of day here in America. Other European countries — all built a power of the people, their independence and right to govern themselves — at the expense of their monarchs.

Simply put, we're more independent when a king can't "lord it over us." Over the last eight centuries, as every freedom we won came at the expense of *sovereign* kings, so we became more sovereign over our own lives!

The other trend over the last few centuries started when a German monk/scholar named Martin Luther tacked 95 points for discussion to the door of the Wittenberg Cathedral.[12] Since then, the Pope's *sovereignty* has been under attack from all of the Protester (Protestant) factions. Even today, in the Roman Catholic Church, many do not see his pronouncements[13] as from God like followers used to see them.

What is common to both trends? We tend to resist anyone saying they are sovereign over us. Period.

We suspect; we distrust any government that holds too much power. We suspect and distrust a religion that tells us to send our treasures ahead to heaven and itself flaunts earthly trappings of money, power and corruption.

We don't want anyone lording it over us; and herein lies the rub: we resist lords be they in government *or in religion*. That makes this book's topic hard — challenging for most, if not all of our readers.

We like to be in charge. We want to be in control. We want to hold the reins in our lives. Although the word sovereign has ***two***

---

[12] It was the eve of All Saints Day, October 31, 1517.

[13] Papal Bulls is the official term.

I want you to see Me

spheres — independence and supremacy — we tend to confuse them and reject *both* spheres. We want to be in control. You might say; we want to be God.

This crashes us smack up against God's offer for salvation and new life.

In America for two centuries revivalists have talked endlessly of Jesus as Savior.[14] They preach that we all can enter a relationship with Jesus as Savior if *we choose* to do so, if *we want* it, if *we desire* so. Using that thinking, Billy Graham admitted that about one in four people who came forward at his public crusades to *accept* Christ as Savior *actually follow through* to start a new life in Christ. The italicized words place so much on our whim, don't they?

That was God's plan? Could He intend for many to think that they make good starts, and few finish the race? Do you think God intends for anyone to take a first taste, and not stay for the main course, much less dessert?

We make a case of how far from truth this thinking is: that the Bible might teach anyone comes to Christ at his own whim, rather than as Christ decides. More than anything we say or do — it is Him, God, who chooses us, rather than we who choose Him.

Consider Jesus' parable of the sower and the seed.

"Once a man went out to sow corn. As he scattered the seed in the field, some of it fell along the path ... and the birds ate it up. Some fell on rocky ground, sprouted, and dried up because the soil had no moisture. Some seed fell among thorn bushes, which grew and choked them. And some seeds fell in good soil; the plants grew and produced corn, 100 grains each."(GNT)[15]

---

[14] Many historians date the rise of "revival" preaching to Charles Finney. In Hankins, Barry. *The Second Great Awakening and the Transcendentalists.* Westport, CN: Greenwood Press, 2004: 137. Interestingly Finney stressed Christ as Savior, rejecting Presbyterian theology stressing God's sovereignty.

[15] Luke 8:5ff.

Begin Where God Began

Hard. This truth is harder than the ground in the parable. It was so hard that the disciples even asked Jesus to interpret it. Jesus explained that the seed in differing places represents people hearing God's Word. Of four reactions; three were bad, tragic even.

Hear our plea in an analogy. We married amazing women, who we love dearly. Imagine that a couple is talking late at night, and she says, "I've discovered a lump in my breast."

No possible response exists for a husband who loves his wife than to say, "We must make a doctor's appointment immediately. We will get to the truth of this. We will face it together." No loving response begins with, "It's probably nothing" or "I don't know...."

Love only abides truth. Love wants truth. Do you want truth, even if it takes you down a notch? Whether you are a woman with a lump in her breast, or your best and dearest friend in the world, your wife, has one in hers, do you want truth from a doctor, or some smiling "friend" to banish momentary worries, and leave you to your fate?

The New Testament makes us think twice. Consider the Greek words for *Savior* and *Lord*. Savior (*soteros*) is used almost twenty times in the gospels, Acts and letters. Savior even applies to God the Father a few of those times, not Jesus! Now consider the term that all writers used for Jesus more than all other terms together: Lord (*kurios*) —277 times.[16] The sheer weight of numbers says, "Jesus is Lord." Their life motivation was overwhelmingly following what their **Lord** said. In the face of those numbers, *Savior* seems to have been a perk in the contract for those taking Christ as Lord.

Overwhelmingly the people living and dying for Christ in the first century saw Jesus as Messiah, King, Lord, boss, CEO, benign dictator and beyond any appeal.[17] If He directed them to India, they

---

[16] Vine, W. E. (1958). *Vines Dictionary of Biblical Words*, Thomas Nelson, Nashville TN. Young, R. (1910). *Young's Analytical Concordance of the Bible*. Crossways, NY.

[17] Pelikan, J. (1992). *Jesus through the Centuries, His Place in the History of Culture*. Yale University Press.

I want you to see Me

went. If He chose them to die in a public arena torn by wild animals for sport, they did so as He moved events.[18] In fact, they considered such a death a gift.[19]

However, from that day forward many, many people calling themselves Christian attack, erode, and whittle away at any idea that Jesus is Lord over our decisions and our lives. They resist Jesus as God or sovereign over us, over our souls.

We don't like anyone lording it over us.

SO, you may hate this book. SO, you desperately need this book. The more you hate this book, the more you may desperately need it.

So, take a minute. Pray that He reveals Himself, shows you truth, shows you where you are, and how to live differently since God is sovereign.

Take this trip with us. Hold on to these two nuggets, whatever you believe.

> *Romans 8:28 We know that in all things God works for the good of those who love Him, who have been called according to His purpose.*

> *Philippians 1:6 Being confident of this, that He who began a good work in you will carry it on to completion until the day of Christ Jesus.*

Hold on to the God Who will deliver on these two promises.

---

[18] Athanasius in the arena when asked to denounce Christ at the age of 84.

[19] Several historians show that "martyrdom" was a spiritual gift, like tongues or prophecy.

2

People Who Knew: Traveling Way Beyond Religion

God left sovereignty's snapshots all through the Bible.
Enjoy some of God's family snapshots.

Paul wrote to churches[20] using every image he could to tell Christians we're free — truly free trusting God. The Gospel unshackles us from sin, rules, and traditions. In a Roman Empire where half the population was enslaved, Paul's words thundered like an earthquake.

Paul also lobbed an even more earth shuddering salvo. He pointed to our big hindrance to freedom: *religion*. Paul summed up religion in an odd word — Law. Law because religion for Paul as a Pharisee and a Jew had been to keep 613 laws beyond the Big Ten (Commandments).[21]

So to the Galatian churches he used a legal metaphor.[22] Paul painted a metaphor where Christians start as children on a huge estate. The estate was willed to us by our Dad, but as kids we're too

---

[20] Those churches in Rome's Galatian region are in the eastern region of present day Turkey.
[21] The Mishnah or Oral Tradition was completed during the time of the Maccabees (~ 100 BC). It codified and explained practical applications of the Mosaic Law in 613 Laws.
[22] Galatians 4:17.

I want you to see Me

young to take over! So that we don't blow the estate on the world's biggest Matchbox car collection, or a girlfriend or give it to Bernie Madoff — Dad provided a trustee. This trustee watches over and administrates us. He makes decisions for us, tells us when we get it wrong, and all of this is grooming us for a time when we are old enough and — as heirs — we take over the estate! We outgrow the trustee.

Only when we finally take over are we like "Dad" and in proper relationship to the estate: heirs cum owners.

In beginning our faith, God's trustee for the estate is the Law. The Law — religion — grows us, teaches us right from wrong; what is good; and teaches us what our lives and families need. The Law is a primer for what God expects of us. Religion is a merciless mentor.[23]

Then the Law has done its job. It's done all it can do. Religion has done all it was *intended* to do. It was never intended to change us. It cannot. It will not. No, religion prepares the way for Christ. Only Christ empowers us how to live as an heir of the estate, co-owner with Him.

God's metaphor teaches us religion's place, and hints at God's gracious place beyond religion for us as His children in today's world.

Basically religion hammers us; it shows how we fail God's standard for us. Religion shows us that as Christians we still sin: translated we're still fail*ers*. We're not fail*ures*, but fail*ers*.[24] It is God's grace alone that says even as we've done bad things, (killing, lying) we're still not murderers and liars. Only a sovereign God can look at me if I have killed another and say, "You are not a murderer." If the stunning truth of that eludes you, read it again. Think, "Ted

---

[23] Romans 7:7-8 I wouldn't have known the desire for what others have if the Law had not said, *"Don't desire what others have."* But sin seized the opportunity and used this commandment to produce all kinds of desires in me. Sin is dead without the Law.

[24] Our thanks to Mike Yaconelli, founding editor of *The Wittenberg Door,* where we first saw this term to explain God's grace to us.

People Who Knew: Traveling Way Beyond Religion

Bundy. Jeffrey Dahmer."[25] None of us are righteous. Translated again — we all need Jesus — to take us beyond religion into: into what?

God used Paul to push the Galatians (and us) to move beyond our proctor, religion, to become heirs of God's Kingdom (along with Jesus!).

Maybe that's not strong enough. Paul used other words for religion:[26] slavery and bondage. He points beyond religion (slavery) to where "Christ has set us free. So stand firm and don't submit to the bondage of slavery (religion) again."

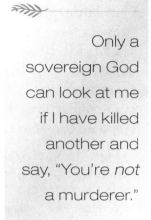

Only a sovereign God can look at me if I have killed another and say, "You're *not* a murderer."

Religion brings bondage. Atheists agree. Religion spreads slavery. Being good in a religion where rule-keeping depends on us more than God, is not God's plan for this universe. It will not work like that here. Garden of Eden, Tower of Babel, all the religions in the Bible — all of them — impose bondage no less than Egyptian slavery imposed bondage on Israelites.

All religions are slavery, no matter how meaningful or real they seem. God intended them to only take you so far. You must move out into a freedom beyond religion to breathe in God and His sovereignty.

So, does God expect us to be good in religion? One, God holds no expectations for anyone's success[27] without Jesus.[28] The Cross

---

[25] Bundy and Dahmer tortured, murdered, and were despicable beyond words. Both also professed Christ as Lord in prison. Bundy before execution had communion with James and Shirley Dobson. Dahmer was executed by other prisoners when they no longer feared him.

[26] Galatians 5:1ff.

[27] Romans 3:21-23.

[28] Moses preached sermons in Deuteronomy before the Israelites took the Promised Land to foretell their falling away from God and going into slavery in far countries (Assyria and Babylon). God knew they would crash and burn.

I want you to see Me

says we can't be good without God. God knew we would need Christ's death and salvation back in the Garden of Eden.[29] Okay, He knew before the Garden of Eden. Two, we don't do good to get God's saving love or His attention. Get the order right. Love and trust God *first*. He provides salvation and gives life *first*. Then we do amazing things. Then when you fail to do amazing things, God uses even your failing(s) to work in you, to complete you. Only sovereign God can use your failings to complete you.

Do we all fail? The Bible says so. In fact a great Christian, Paul, expresses our failings like this:

> *I know that good doesn't live in me — that is, in my body. The desire to do good is inside of me, but I can't do it. I don't do the good that I want to do, but I do the evil that I don't want to do.[30] I'm a miserable human being! Who will deliver me from this dead corpse?[31]*

If we are as honest as Paul then we will admit — we all harbor a treasure trove of failings. And here it gets interesting. Religion only has two ways to deal with true, deep failing. First, it glosses over failures to say, "It doesn't count," or "It is no big deal." How tragic. Our guilt over what we did is already painful, so someone seeing our broken heart and damaged relationship who says, "That does not count," or "It's no big deal," doesn't help. My broken heart aches. My damaged relationship pains me. Religion downplaying the reality of my damaged soul does no good.

Second, religion gives me more things to try out. Endlessly. "Well, you should try this. Here, take two quiet times and call me in the morning."

"You should go to church or confession more! You should *fill in the blank*." In time, we begin to know that we can't fill in enough

---

[29] Ephesians 1:4 God chose us before the creation of the world. Revelation 13:8 God had for all intents and purposes slain Jesus before the foundation of this world.

[30] Romans 7:18-19.

[31] Romans 7:24.

People Who Knew: Traveling Way Beyond Religion

blanks. There is no scheme, no penance or seven-steps-to-clearing-my conscience in any religion that can clean my conscience. If nothing else draws me beyond religion then nothing pushes my festering soul beyond its bondage.

Only Jesus offers forgiveness to start over, and moreover, forgiveness to *continue* — even beyond religion. Forgiveness to continue is beyond-belief-important.

Have you failed so big that you could never have conceived of doing something so bad when you were young? You would never have believed that you could hurt so many people as deeply as you have? You would never have believed you could betray someone and wound them so terribly. How could you even conceive that you could let down so many people so close to you?[32]

Did you fail that badly after professing Christ? So you knew better. Doesn't that make it a thousand times worse? You see, it did not take nearly as much forgiving, or as much cleansing for your little heart as a beginner sinner — as a child — as it does for you as a grown-up failer.

Religious pictures that served us well in Vacation Bible School or in a children's church program don't work as well now, do they? Hear the challenge. Did you outgrow God or did you outgrow religion's *picture* of God that we give children? Did you outgrow Christ or your *picture* of Christ that you loved as a child? Do you now need a more grownup picture of God and Christ?

Beyond religion — do you need God? Beyond religion, do you need a bigger God than you had growing up as a kid? How will it look? How will it look if you cease believing it is all about you, and begin to believe that it is all about God? What does that look like? As we mentioned above, how does an heir of God's Kingdom act? What sort of freedom does that afford us like Paul says later in his

---

[32] There is no righteous person, not even one. There is no one who understands. There is no one who looks for God. Romans 3:10-11.

I want you to see Me

circular to the Galatian churches? What has God scripted for those who know His sovereignty best?

What has He sovereignly scripted — indeed?

Let's view some family snapshots of people who are *in the groove* or playing *in the faith zone* of a sovereign God big enough to handle — anything.

Whisper that to yourself: "Anything."

Sovereignty family snapshot #1: Noah

In ancient times, a terrible judgment was coming over the world. God was about to wash away most of the evidence of man and his sin. Here Snapshot #1 shows a man who knew God's sovereignty.

In sovereignty Family Snapshot #1 we see Noah posing with his sons after a long day's work in front of a huge ark: a boat large enough to hold the world's flora and fauna. The world will be drenched in rain and flood. In the photo, we see Noah has built his ark miles from water. As we interview him we find he has never seen a rain shower. He built his ark on a hill having never seen rain.

Will he live to see animals from around the globe take their assigned places on an ark? Will he live to see the world covered in water and God finally beach that ark on a mountain as the water recedes? Yes, but today with his sons (he was no great preacher — only his family believed him) he is building an ark according to God's blueprint. Way beyond any world religion, and they had all grown twisted — Noah did what God told him even as his neighbors laughed.

God chose Noah, who trusted his family's lives in God's will, no matter how crazy the adventure! God worked it all for their good. A lot of people drowned. Noah built an ark in a sovereign God's will and God brought his family through the judgment. Noah looks relaxed in the photo, doesn't he?

Sovereignty family snapshot #2: Abram

We see an old man shoo away vultures in stark relief due to a setting sun. Vultures are gathering because the grizzled old man killed some large animals, hacked them in half, and spread the halves on either side of a little space. He has shooed vultures and other birds away for hours, and now finally, the sun sets.

Years ago, this old man was in a temple of a moon god when God interrupted his worship and told him to bring his family to this Promised Land.[33] Just like that.

And now Abram sits shooing off ever bolder vultures in a promised land God is showing him: tired, hot, and a little shaky after not eating or drinking when God said to kill the animals and make a sacred patch of earth with their blood.

Abram was ready to renew his *relationship* with the invisible God, so he did all God said. He killed animals to renew his covenant in a promised land he was shown, and for which he had no heir. This was so far past any religion; Abe must have been reeling inside, just a bit.

Does Abram look a little foolish out there? Sure. You bet. Even the vultures wondered about this guy. Is God working in him and changing him? You bet your life.

Will God actually fulfill His promise(s) to Abram and Sarai? The Jews, and the Christians and the Muslims all resoundingly say, "Yes!"

God changed all equations for religion with Abram because the old man was faithful, at least occasionally. As the old man shooed scavengers away from sacred ground between cut up animals, God showed what it looked like to live beyond religion — in Abraham.

---

[33] The major worship centers in Ur and in Haran were Temples to the moon god. Some scholars link this to the same god that Mohammed told the pagans was his god as well.

I want you to see Me

If Abraham was made righteous because of his actions, he would have had a reason to brag, but not in front of God. What does the scripture say? Abraham had faith in God, and [his faith] was credited to him as righteousness.[34]

God gave Abram faith. So Abram could act as God directed, even if it felt a little crazy. Faith trumps trying to be good. God credits faith acts as righteousness. God said so.

Beyond any moon-god-religion, Abram was charting new ground. Abram walked way past religion in faith to follow the sovereign God who held Abram's (and our) future in His hands. It's funny. Abraham followed God way beyond religion, and now three religions all claim him as founder.

Did Abram fail his wife[35] and son?[36] Yes. Big time. But God moved the accounting system beyond Abram's being good (religion) to Abram's faith in God. It went beyond Abram's morality or goodness. It was, all about God. God counted Abram's faith as righteousness.

Catch that. Beyond religion, God counts *our faith in Him as sovereign* as more than morality and as more than ethics — as righteousness.

Sovereignty family snapshot #3: Joshua

There behind the priests carrying the ark and blowing horns; and in front of all the soldiers, isn't that Moses' aide de camp, Joshua, marching around Jericho for the seventh time on the seventh day? Look closer. Is he staring at Jericho's city walls that look so impregnable?[37] He is about to tell trumpets to blow long and

---

[34] Romans 4:12.

[35] Genesis 12:11ff when he pawned off his wife as his sister to Pharaoh. Genesis 20:1ff when he pawned her off as his sister to King Abimelech of Gerar.

[36] He kicked out his first son, Ishmael to die in the desert with his mother, Hagar. Genesis 16:1ff. He took Isaac up a mountain, fully intending to sacrifice him back to God. Genesis 22:1ff.

[37] Joshua 6:1ff.

then to have the silent people shout — so God can drop this city's impregnable walls and they will run in and take the city.

Right. Sure.

Joshua scans again for and sees a red sash flapping idly in the breeze, hanging out of Rahab's window in the wall and he smiles slightly. Can a sovereign God erase all but her small part of a city wall as people shout? Will Rahab and her family be Jericho's sole survivors tonight?

Yes. Tonight the Israelites will mop up the city. Two spies will bring Rahab and her kin to meet Joshua. He'll see that Salmon can't take his eyes off Rahab.[38] A fear of the Israelites will spread like a stench through the region.

But now, without ever having seen God drop a city wall or even a tent when people shout, Joshua is moving from trusting Moses' God, to believing God Himself. This is obviously not about whether people can shout loud to shatter stone. No, this plan to take this city is about God. It is about believing God is sovereign over nations who hate Him, cities that reject Him — and sovereign over stone. Joshua gives the order.

Joshua started small, waiting on Moses. He watched Moses. Followed him anywhere God allowed. He learned that God was way beyond a local god: sovereign over Pharaohs, Red Seas, and other nations as Moses' aide de camp.

When Joshua gives the order for the long trumpet blasts followed by the people shouting and grabbing their swords, he is placing everything he is, everything he knows in the hands of sovereign God.

He did not end up looking foolish.

---

[38] They married and had a son named Boaz. You may have heard of him in Ruth's story.

I want you to see Me

Sovereignty family snapshot #4: David

There, wading in a brook hunting five smooth stones like you skip across a lake's surface: see a pudgy teen? He needs five smooth, aerodynamic stones to sink into the skulls of five giants.

An hour ago, David was pointing at Goliath who seemed far away. The boy/man was trembling with rage, asking his brothers — they were all older as he was the runt of the litter — the kid was asking everyone in their hearing, "How can you stand here and listen to that, that uncircumcised blasphemer!?"[39]

Minutes ago, he stared up at King Saul, who realized this teen looked even sillier in armor. Now as the kid waded in a brook to gather stones for his sling, David saw Israel's army, the army of the Lord Almighty shifting from foot to foot: ready to run for their lives. He heard no encouragement, just gasps as men saw that Saul had let a mere boy step up to battle Goliath.

Their gasps said this would be tragic and quick. And Goliath? Insanely insulted! He angrily raved spittle on his beard at this affront to his manhood.

Belief in sovereign God looks like David picking up five smooth stones in a brook, since he heard this big clown has four backups. It will be a long day if he must kill all five. The boy follows a script that he alone is free to follow. As everyone else cowers; slaves to religion, to fear, to how the world works — David follows his calling— God scripting this as if David was the apple of His eye.

Years from now will David build God a nation? Yes. Years from now will he fall and fail? Yes. Others have catalogued his life well. Did David see all of that as God working deep in him, culling out what God didn't want in him? Read the Psalms. They answer, "Yes!" His confidence was that a sovereign God was working His plan in David just as He does in all His children.

---

[39] 1 Samuel 17:26.

People Who Knew: Traveling Way Beyond Religion

In minutes by the way, he kills the giant, cuts off his head with his own sword and keeps his sword.

But right now, he is living as an heir of God's Kingdom. In the snapshot, he is but a kid who spent lonely nights singing to God with a harp, tending sheep, and killing a stray lion or bear as needed for no one else to see but God. And he freely loads a slingshot as he runs to get a closer shot at this foulmouthed behemoth because he can't abide this clown blaspheming Israel's sovereign God.

Want some more? The more snapshots you see, the more you see that the entire Bible is about all of us reaching a place where we realize: it is all about God and His plan for planet earth. Everyone in the book comes to see that God alone is God, and that His Word is inalterable. Unshakable. Some like Moses and Joshua see that as God's blessed children. Others — Pharaoh and Goliath — see God as sovereign only in dying lost without Him.

Sovereignty family snapshot #5: Esther

She looks stunning! Look at the eyes and face! This Esther won a beauty contest from all of Persia (girls from India to Egypt, from the Sudan to Russia) in order to be named queen. Esther was Jewish, but following uncle Mordecai's advice she kept that hidden until now.

Haman has amassed enough power and hate to exterminate all the Jews. Sound like Hitler? Mordecai tells Esther that it may be for such a time as this that she won the beauty contest and has the King's ear — but significant risks — history works against her![40]

Esther sends word from her palace calling all Jews to pray and fast as she does so with her harem girls. She is the only Jewess in her harem! Now the girls and the eunuchs all know who she is.

---

[40] Esther is queen because the previous queen would not come when the king summoned her. NOW Esther will do the reverse of this by going to see the king when she has not been summoned! Esther 1:1-22.

I want you to see Me

In the snapshot, Esther stands before her king who hasn't summoned her, and if he does not have her killed for breaching his power — or for being a Jewess — she will plead for her people's lives! Now, stepping into court as the king sees her, before he accepts or rejects her, before we know how her story plays out — she plays her part to play in sovereign God's plan to save His people just as all of God's children do, every day.

In two days, God will use her to save the Jews, but stepping into the court, awaiting her king's glance and possible rejection and death, she looks stunning doesn't she?

Sovereignty family snapshot #6: Ezra

A rabbi, Ezra, stands with a desert to his back and his country's treasury piled before him. Ezra bragged on God. He would protect His Jews returning to Jerusalem carrying the wealth the Babylonians had stripped from them. See the Ahava canal over his shoulder? See leading Jews screaming at him? They rave because they could have had the King's cavalry as an escort across the badlands, and they won't because big shot Ezra bragged that God was sovereign over badlands and brigands. Who needs an escort!?

Ezra looks pretty peaceful standing in front of raving people, though.

We could view many more snapshots of people who got it: Ruth, Elijah and Elisha, Nehemiah, Naomi, and Miriam all got it — God is sovereign over all time, all nations, and all people.

Paul added that our best hope beyond religion is that God is righteous.[41] God carries on an ongoing conversation at some level with every person who ever lived.[42] God always, ultimately does

---

[41] Romans chapters 1-3.

[42] Creation, the orderliness of Creation (science), law, Law/Torah and Conscience are means by which God talks to us all. Romans 1-3.

right by Himself. Remember, that is far, far beyond us doing right (failers all) or God doing *right by us* (that would be hell). *God does right by Himself.* That's the ultimate definition of sovereign. God does what God would do, all other factors notwithstanding. All other factors fail.

Translated: God the Potter, who was shaping Noah, Abram, Moses, Joshua, David, Esther and Ezra — was also handing them snapshots of Himself. He wanted them to see Him behind the circumstances He used to shape them, to show them His sovereign plan. God didn't hand out religious photos of a tabernacle, temple, commandments or an altar. Sovereign God helped them see Him in the events of their lives.

All of them exercised freedom to make choices as long as their choices didn't interfere with what God was doing, what God was shaping in them!

Oh, and Ezra made it back to Jerusalem safe and sound, just as his sovereign God scripted it.

3

Two-faced

Most Christians salute the sovereignty of God, but believe in the sovereignty of man.
—R.C. Sproul

E = MC2

What Einstein captured in that equation still amazes. He parsed over fifty other physicists' and mathematicians' works, and honed them into one, astonishing equation. Third graders memorize it. Most adults can't comprehend it. Books cram libraries based on it. Physicists start here to theorize about our cosmos. This font of genius inspires generations of scientists.

Paul wrote a Biblical equivalent in three verses to friends at Ephesus.

It is by grace you have been saved, through faith — and this is not from yourselves, it is God's gift — not by works, so that no one can boast. For we are God's handiwork, created in Christ Jesus to do good works, which God prepared in advance for us to do.[43]

See our faith from Father accesses His grace to save us. See also: faith is a gift. So is Grace. Not from us. God made us. He created

---

[43] Ephesians 2:810.

I want you to see Me

us (in Christ) to do good works He prepared in advance. He gave us faith to access the grace to do any of it.

Father gives faith	Father gives grace	It's not us	We're God's handiwork	Created in Christ	To do good works	That the Father prepared in advance for us.

Every piece of it — grace, faith, works — all comes from God.

Every piece of it — grace, faith, works — is intertwined like quarks, electrons, and the four forces intertwine matter.

Every piece of it flows sweeping, directing life and history. Put it another way. I do no good work God didn't set up for me. I do no good work His grace did not bring to me. Even my faith to do the work is a gift.

It is all about Him.

Like Einstein, Paul synthesized the work of those who went before him: men like Moses. Hear Moses' last sermon.

* God circumcises your hearts and your descendants' hearts, so that you may love Him with all your heart and with all your soul, and live.

** You will again obey the Lord and follow all His commands.

*** Then God will make you most prosperous in all the work of your hands and in the fruit of your womb, the young of your livestock and your crops. The Lord will again delight in you and make you prosperous, just as He delighted in your ancestors,

As we obey the Lord ... and turn to Him with all our heart and with all our soul.[44] See some things to see in these verses.

---

[44] Deuteronomy 30:6-10.

Two-faced

* **God** circumcises[45] our hearts. We can't. We can't *be* or *become* good enough. We're not honest with ourselves or God.

** **God** enables us to obey His commands.

*** **The Lord** delights in us and makes us prosperous.

Then God addresses OUR RESPONSE.

We keep His commands and decrees.

Did you miss it? God pours out all good things in one sweeping motion to keep us serving and growing. God creates works for us *ahead of time*! If we ask Him to do anything, God had answers in play before we were born. He had to have the prep work in motion before we thought to ask! All of our might and our wisdom works with what He already has given us.

E = MC2 is a lot like God's sovereignty = (grace*faith*works)

How to respond to such sweeping truth pointing us onward? Ambivalence or worse; we become two-faced. ***Two-faced*** means. Insincere and deceitful. Synonyms: deceitful, double-dealing, hypocritical, **Janus-faced,** backstabbing, false, fickle, untrustworthy, duplicitous, deceiving, dissembling, dishonest.

God calls it delusional.[46]

Living as if life is about us, brings conflict. Conflict spawns anxiety, fear, and guilt. We've created a spiritual shorthand. We say, "My lower nature conflicts with my higher nature." or "I was conflicted," or "this is God's permissive will" or "God helps those who help themselves."[47] We try taking over while ignoring the universe's underlying structure — God is in control.

---

[45] Circumcision is a physical picture of a spiritual principle. God cuts away the gunk between our hearts and His Spirit so that we may know His presence and obey.

[46] Jeremiah 10:14-15.

[47] Benjamin Franklin.

I want you to see Me

Why are we two-faced? Well-meaning people train us to think like this. Religious people model it and commend it to us in sermons and teachings.

Consider pastors. They wholly agree — God is sovereign! But stepping up to preach a mystery occurs. Pastors hope to deliver sermons that make sense to us. Privately espousing God's sovereignty, but not preaching it can only be explained by — two-facedness.

We dialogued with pastors. We constructed one out of many interviews and we call him "Bill." Bill may describe your preaching pastor where you attend church.

Tom: let me say Gary can be a pain. ☺ His successes as a trial lawyer have honed a keen, precise ear when listening. I listen globally, missing discrepancies that win or lose Gary's cases. His merciless training makes him a great trial lawyer. So he hears what I miss when listening to pastors from whom we constructed our composite "Bill."

"Bill" successfully pastors and leads a sharp staff. His denomination trained him at a world-class seminary. In seminaries professors may espouse God's sovereign nature, yet fail to uphold His sovereignty in teaching. While paying lip service to God's sovereignty, they unconsciously burden us to complete ourselves — for us to finish the work God began in us.

On Sundays as worship teams sit down, pastors preach. Precisely here is the onset of two-facedness. Speaking privately a pastor who espoused —

- God is *absolutely* supreme in directing history — our lives —
- That scripture bears witness to this throughout —
- That God is unshakably sovereign in the Bible —

Bill starts preaching and rugged American, self-determination emerges. Like a Greek actor, he puts on another face to preach that we *let God* work in us, we *let God* call us to obedience. What? Almighty God needs our permission?

46

Two-faced

See how odd it sounds when pointed out? Bill even preaches this after agreeing over lunch that God can do and does do what He "jolly well pleases!"

Try saying these aloud:

"I must let God bring up the sun tomorrow."

"I will let God bring that front with snow!"

"I can let go and let God cause birds to migrate."

"I will let God keep me from cancer today."

"I won't let God bring a tornado."

Really? You can change those? Can you *say* them aloud? No. We know His power and control over nature, right?

Hang on. Hear why this shadows our pulpits today. You may say, "Birds or snow don't have free will, yet humans do."

So we are at the crux of our discussion. Or open questioning people, God's chosen desperately need to hear this.

We desperately need to hear: we have no free will. Satan markets that distortion of scripture, even to highly intelligent people. But it's not based on scripture. Scripture is clear: God never gives up control to anyone.[48]

---

[48] Jer.18:6 "O house of Israel, can I not do with you as this potter has done?" declares the Lord. "Behold, like the clay in the potter's hand, so are you in My hand."
Jeremiah 29:11 "I know the plans I have for you, declares the Lord, plans for welfare (Or peace) and not for evil, to give you a future and a hope."
2 Chronicles 36:17 So [God] brought up against (His people) a king of the Chaldeans.
2 Chronicles 36:22-23 the Lord stirred up the spirit of Cyrus king of Persia, so that he made a proclamation throughout his kingdom ...:"The Lord, the God of heaven, has given me all the kingdoms of the earth, and he has charged me to build Him a house at Jerusalem, which is in Judah."
Jer.10:12 Do not let your heart be troubled. His purpose for our lives will be fulfilled.
Isaiah 46:9-10 ...remember the things of old. I am God, and there is no other; I am God, and there is none like Me, declaring the end from the beginning and from ancient times things not yet done, saying, "My counsel shall stand, and I will accomplish all my purpose,"
Psalm 33:10-11 The Lord brings the counsel of the nations to nothing; He frustrates the plans of the peoples.
His counsel stands forever, the plans of His heart to all generations.
Proverbs 19:21 Many are the plans in the mind of a man, but it is the Lord's purpose that will stand.

I want you to see Me

You say, "I can do anything I want tonight! I can honor God or do any crazy thing(s) I choose, but I choose!" Hear how childish it sounds; "I can do any rebellious or stupid thing I want!" Sure, but all you choose tonight, is already in God's accounting of your life. He steals nothing from you, but choosing is so integral to being a self—no matter how stupidly we choose — that it makes us arch our backs and bristle. Stay with us. Let's connect the dots.

Two-facedness is so prevalent and seduces so many church leaders in so many forms that most of us are blind to it.

Why does the epidemic go viral as pastors touch our free will? How is God sovereign over an entire universe: nature, angels, nations and weather — but He trips up on our free will? Why here do pastors forget scriptures telling us that God directs the steps of the righteous — His children?[49]

Remember, God has promised to finish His good work in us.[50] How can He finish it if we can use a free will to nullify it? How could God put in us anything that might place us outside of His mercy, of His devotion to us?

Pastor Bill on Monday: "Gary, we're on the same page on sovereignty." But defending Sunday's sermon's double talk he says, "In my mind if I say, 'Let God do such and such,' I don't feel that I diminish His sovereignty." Really?

Bill continues, "God can override anything in my life." So, we initiate. God must then override? God initiated. He created the world. Did He then stop initiating?

Bill: "God has a plan to perform His will in my life. Yes, He's working out that plan, but I do have the opportunity to join Him in

---

[49] Jeremiah 10:23 Lord, I know that people's lives are not their own; it is not for them to direct their steps.

[50] Philippians 1:6 being confident of this, that He who began a good work in you will carry it on to completion until the day of Christ Jesus.

Two-faced

that work and not struggle against Him." (That's God's sovereign gift, not of us, lest we should boast.[51])

Our individualism seduces pastors to conform messages to us. Also, our rugged self-determination blocks our understanding God's sovereignty.

Gary's friend Keith graduated from a denominational university and ministered for years before building a motivational business. One evening he brought Gary a documentary: *The Secret.* He excitedly played it and as it finished he jumped up to ask, "What do you think?"

Gary replied, "Keith, if you want to embrace or follow New Age teaching or thinking, this will fit you perfectly."

Keith pushed back, "But Gary this is spiritually based."

Gary, "Keith, it's shaped really well to give that impression." I then pointed to several of the film's ideas — New Age concepts — and showed how the writers and editors artfully wrapped ideas in spirituality. Spirituality is only one threat in a long line of possible replacements for scriptural truth.

I paused; not certain whether to push further. Keith's face wrinkled in interest. He anticipated more. I said, "Keith, I think you will pursue this film's 'revelation,' and I further sense that right now you want it more than you want the things of God."

I paused again. It's hard to say, harder to hear: "Keith, I even suggest you go with it; but as God's child, you'll be back, after He uses it to work in you what He wants to do. You'll be back. No question, and when you're back — black and blue — you'll be more perfected for God's purposes in your life."

Is that not what life is about? Scripture is clear. *Life is about God using us for His purposes and perfecting us for the Kingdom.*

---

[51] Philippians 2:89.

I want you to see Me

My friend Keith's surprised face still burns in my memory today. I had mentored Keith for years — and not that he needed to hear me say it, I gave him a go ahead to rebel? Why? Because rebellion was in Keith, just as Jonah brandished his brand of rebellion. Talking to Jonah dockside, awaiting his boat to Tarshish, would have wasted Jonah's and God's time.

Keith wanted a power of self will. He hoped to magically call out words and make them real. That night he wanted power more than God, so I entrusted Keith to our Father to work in him. God would perform His will in Keith. God would use *even this* to perfect him. Simply. It is not so hard to grasp is it?

Did I give him a license to sin? I have no license to give. God holds **all** licenses, and He never glosses over our continually sinning, and He will[52] *use even that* (**all** things!) for our good. Can it get any more beautiful?

We don't even have to fear these side trips. Many times, God has charted them and knows how He will use them decades from now to perfect us.

Keith's next chapter encourages me. He wasn't gone long. On returning he was more perfected in Christ. He even brought it up later, sharing how much God taught him *in his desert*. Keith now knows, that God works His will in us, period! He's perfecting us for His Kingdom. Sovereign means — our King is accomplishing in His Kingdom all He knows is needed. Even Keith's side trip to *new age desert*, was part of the King's perfecting process.

Hard to believe? Don't like it? Have challenges? Read on.

A case of biblical two-facedness

Let's follow a confirmed two-faced man: Jonah. Ask this. Did God even use a prophet's 'side' trip to perfect His image in him? — Even as Jonah's side trip arose from his rebellion?

---

[52] Romans 8:28.

Two-faced

Jonah's sermons are soaked in God's sovereign judgment, but as *Jonah's personal* sovereign God, God should hate whoever Jonah hated, right? Jonah hated Assyrians. As a Jew, *his* God should hate Assyrians, and of all Assyrians, God should especially hate Ninevites: rulers of Assyria. Armies from Nineveh slaughtered and raped God's people in the Northern Kingdom, marching the survivors naked into oblivion with fish hooks in their noses. These very Ninevites could destroy the remaining Jews in Judah as well.

God tasked Jonah to preach His judgment *in* Nineveh! Jonah should have jumped at a chance to spew venom on the capital's streets, scaring children, and shocking prideful politicians. What a dream assignment for a prophet!

But Jonah booked a boat in the opposite direction of Nineveh to the known world's other edge, and swung below decks to hide. Hiding from a sovereign God: that's challenging.

A gale tossed his ship like a cork, only this cork was sinking. Did God smile as Jonah tried to hide? A roiling storm caused the crew to jettison cargo, making the trip a loss.

Winds shrieked louder, and sailors rolled dice to find whom the gods were angry at onboard. All watch judgment roll with the dice. Jonah saves time saying, "Put me against the rest of the ship." The dice roll — Jonah — who makes it easy, "Throw me overboard."

They do. Storm stops. Jonah should have drowned, but a God sovereign over biology does this — Jonah gets swallowed by a fish and lives. In the fish. Under the sea.

Gross, right?

God is stewing something in the fish. Jonah furiously spews at God why he hates the Nineveh assignment after two more dark days — and Jonah's anger is precisely where God is working in him.

You see the prophet in that black belly **knew** God is the sort of God that if Jonah hit Nineveh thundering God's remorseless

I want you to see Me

judgment of those horrid, heathen conquerors; that *if* they turned to God — and this was unthinkable to Jonah — God would forgive them. God would let the hated conquerors live.

God's love is like that. Infuriating. God's sovereign love often infuriates us. The Jonahs in the world don't hate bad people getting bad things. They do hate it when bad people get God's forgiveness and blessings.

After all, how can Jonah's (our) sovereign God show love and mercy to undeserving people, to a capital city, to a nation living in sin? It made Jonah mad.

God, sovereign God is always stretching us to see as He sees. Gary: In 2000 I attended a three week, Jerry Spence lawyer boot camp in Wyoming. The promos said: "come with an openness to 'think outside the box.'" The worst I could do was enjoy stunning scenery with forty seven others who understood my work.

In our first session in groups of eight, we were to reveal what we had never or would rarely ever reveal. Ricky shared he was an atheist. My walls went up. I would have nothing to do with him: he didn't believe in my Father. Then, in my second group, God impressed me to form a relationship with Cricket: a looming, powerful black lady.

We rotated through more groups of eight every four days.

I questioned, "God, if it's about the black issue, how about Tyron? He's well groomed, black, and deferential."

God pressed me, "No, Cricket." Oddly, all three black people on the retreat were in my second group. I countered, "God if it's the black and/or female deal, what about Sharon? She's attractive, nice, and young."

Again, "No, Cricket." Being unusually quick if God excludes all other possibilities, I said, "Okay." I reached out to Cricket — who

Two-faced

returned not only no response, she totally rejected me. I continued reaching to her.

We rotated groups. Cricket passed to another group so I sought her out at lunch and in the evening with the same result — total rejection. One night we drove to Dubois to hear a live band in a club. I asked Cricket to dance. Reluctantly, begrudgingly she accepted after heckling from the others.

Barriers began to fade.

Days later my roommate came in saying a black lady, "the large one," really let it all hang out in her psychodrama session. He related that she was a lesbian, and she told it "all."

That blew me further aback. Lying on my bunk, I sighed silently, "God, I can't do this."

God replied, "Why not?"

"God, everyone knows Cricket leads a lesbian lifestyle. If I continue to reach out to her, to form a bond, people will think that I approve of her lifestyle."

God responded, "*That's* none of your business!!" I took minutes to absorb that. God was shattering my paradigm.

I connected the dots: "Well, God if that is the case then I can also reach out to Ricky, the atheist." I hope God smiles in the silences. So I did. Day by day, lunch by lunch and dinner by dinner; I enjoyed them.

Days later I was walking alone as someone ran to catch me. Ricky ran up catching his breath to say, "Mr. Richardson, when I grow up I want to be just like you." Sovereign God rocked my boat. I had reached out to Ricky for one week. I showed him God's love, and he wanted to be "just like me." What a change for us both!

On our last day in a group session on racism, I asked Cricket if she felt a bond with me. Clear eyed, she smiled, "I do." I told the group I didn't grow up with black people. None attended church

I want you to see Me

or college with me, and even though I had represented some; I never formed a bond with a black person. I had to say, "Thank you for this privilege."

Sovereign God worked His change deep in me. The lesson has lasted, in how I view people "who live in sin." I am a little less two-faced here, listening for what the Lord wants, rather than how I was raised in religion to think and act.

Hear again Jonah's sovereign God's charge: It's not your business. You love them. Tell them God's Truth.

The Jonahs don't hate bad people getting bad things. They hate bad people getting God's goodness! If we all get hell for being bad; okay, all sad. But some very bad people get God's forgiveness, His love, and His best. How infuriating to the Jonahs! And maybe to you.

Our sovereign God shows love and mercy to people we hate!? Yes. God let Jonah stew in that, literally, cruising deep in the Mediterranean.

Guess in what direction the fish was headed? Go ahead and laugh: Nineveh.

God used Jonah's run for Tarshish, storm, and fish time to craft a new thing in him: an obedient prophet. God used Jonah's two-facedness — I believe in Sovereign God, but I can still run from Him. God used his hatred of the Ninevites, the ship, the storm, the fish. God chartered Jonah's 'side' trip — all of it.

Read the story. Jonah preached. Nineveh, the king, all responded to God's message. Jonah stayed furious at God's mercy. His story ends with God still working in Jonah — great success in Nineveh — and uncertainty as to how Jonah turned out. God knew what He was doing in Nineveh. He knew they would respond faster than God's man, Jonah, to God's mercy!

Jonah's lesson. Our lesson: we can obey God and still not align our desires with His desires! Jonah had a front row seat for God's huge revival and missed it all — pouting. How could he preach it

Two-faced

and get it so wrong? How did he miss the two important <u>nots</u> in the following?

> *"It's all about God ——* it's **not** all about me."
> *"God is sovereign ——* **not** if I let Him be so."

God moves us beyond thinking it's all about us. Jonah failed to make the jump.

God is healing our two faces to make one face.

Can I follow steps in *allowing* Sovereign God to use me? Can I choose to align my desires with His known will, His known scriptures? In the Bible, that is called being wise. In fact, the longest Psalm dwells on studying God's Word to align my heart with His purposes.[53]

God has foreknown[54] my every choice. Further, He is directing my steps.[55] My steps either align with God's will or, like Jonah it's my rebellion. God allows my rebelling, using even this for my good — to prefect His image in me. Some Christians call rebellion free will. I wonder: did Jonah thrill to cling to his free will as Nineveh rejoiced and he pouted?

Will you go so far in silly thinking like Jonah? He made it clear he was free to be sad about a vine dying that offered him shade and angry God saved Nineveh. You can hear God, "Yeah, right! Need some sunscreen now that your shade is dead?" How do we miss religion promoting rebellion in God's children as free will? A list of Israel's kings shows how long and how low we can rebel. Their short reigns were hellish. Those kings are your free will poster boys. For each prophet telling God's truth, kings employed paid prophets to counter, slap, and kill the Truth tellers. Paid prophets gave messages we love: "God loves us. Nothing bad is coming. Business outlook is

---

[53] Psalm 119, all 176 verses.

[54] Romans 8:29.

[55] Proverbs 16:9, Proverbs 20:24.

I want you to see Me

great!"[56] Satan sold rebellion as freedom at concession stands in the Jew's temple, and now he uses TV and pulpits.

Name the only person devoid of two-facedness

I (Gary) ask Pastor Bill,[57] "Was Jesus all about doing the Father's will?"

Of course — he answers, "Yes."

I follow: "How unlike a puppet was Jesus?" Two-faced pastors just stare when I ask that.

"Bill, would you rather be God's puppet or 'free' and less like Christ?" The Bills and so many others blink. And stare.

How can Christians fear being a puppet when Jesus (as a man) did quite well doing *only* God's will? Even those who don't consider Jesus as God, still see Him as one of history's truly free people! God never disciplined Jesus because He always acted inside Papa's will, no matter what Jesus felt or thought. We struggle here.

I find more freedom, making my plans and trusting God to direct my path than I ever had before.[58] Do we struggle if we fear discipline? God covered this —

We have all had human fathers who disciplined us and we respected them for it. How much more should we submit to the Father of spirits and live! [Our fathers] disciplined us for a little while as they thought best; but God disciplines us for our good, in order that we may share in His holiness. No discipline seems pleasant at the

---

56   The prophets that countered Jeremiah in Judah's final days and the prophets that countered God's men in Israel's final days were pointedly terrible to the Truth speakers.

57   Again, "Bill" is a composite of pastors, so this conversation happened with many people.

58   This is how Paul lived his life after Christ. Paul made plans and God changed them to steer Paul as God directed. See the entire episode where Paul wanted the visit the Scythians and God kept steering him to finally make landfall on Europe in Philippi.

time, but painful. Later on, however, it produces a harvest of righteousness and peace for those who have been trained by it.[59]

If Jesus is the single-faced doer of God's will, where can we find a champion of two-faced people? Right where you expect, and we all tip our hat to him every January first: Janus the two-faced god of the Romans. January is named for him.

You know January, when the gyms fill with people who are going to lose weight and work out for two, maybe three weeks? When people count days before New Year's resolutions are resoundingly abandoned?

An early etymology for Janus' name came from an ancient scholar: Paul the Deacon. The Greeks definition of Chaos[60] shaped their notion that became the Roman's god Janus.[61]

- Janus had two faces, one looking forward and one backward.

- His two opposing aspects bear the moods of a capricious person.

- Two-faced meant deceitful.

Here we see the quandaries of Christians who are two-faced about God's sovereignty. They fear God is capricious and deceitful. *We* are! That's how we are tempted to use our 'freedom' and so we fear how God might use His. We project our fears on Him. The Roman's projected theirs on to Janus.

Janus arose from a universe of Chaos: an ocean of conflicting whims, hopes, desires and choices with no rhyme or reason to form a rock on which to stand.

---

[59] Hebrews 12:9-11.

[60] Paul found that the Greeks dropped the "h" hiantem, hiare, (be open), from which word Ianus would derive by loss of the initial aspirate. The Greeks put an ['] in front of an "I" to make an "h" sound.

[61] Paulus Diaconius Warnefred, (of Monte Cassino), was a Benedictine monk and historian of the Lombards.

Not so with God who forged order in Genesis 1:1 with His words. Order is why science works, gravity is always true, and we can trust that if things in an experiment worked one way the first time, we can replicate it a second time.

Janus' two-faced universe is chaos. God as sovereign brings order and the two promises to believers we began the book quoting.

We carry two other marks of Janus in our thinking, both may help you understand two-faced responses to God's sovereignty. The first forms the English word *janitor*. Romans sought a god to serve as a janitor: cleaning up their messes.

Janus' other mark is our word *hiatus*: when bands or congress go on a break. And if we project anything on God it is that we know we go on hiatus from following or obeying God, so if life is hard to explain — maybe He did as well.

See the alternative to Jesus' puppet-like obedience is in Janus: two-faced, deceitful, capricious, god as janitor, god on hiatus. The alternative *is* frightening.

An exporter of ultimate two-facedness

The world sells a "freedom" over God.

Gary studied L. Ron Hubbard and his Church of Scientology in prepping nine cases against Narconon, Scientology's arm using Hubbard's teachings at "rehab" centers, this one a few miles from Tulsa in Pittsburgh County.

Hubbard is a case of taking two-faced to diabolical lengths.

According to his son, Nibs, Hubbard aimed to be "the most powerful being in the universe." He wanted to "found a religion like Moses and Jesus." Hubbard's medical director described him as having traits of: "paranoid personality. Delusions of grandeur. Pathological lying . . . and malignant narcissism." He further

Two-faced

termed him "a highly insecure individual protecting himself with aggressive grandiosity, disavowal of any and every need from others, antisocial orientation and a heady and toxic mix of rage / anger / aggression / violence and paranoia."[62]

Freedom from God creates — creates what, exactly?

Hubbard published *Dianetics* with zero science training to sell 18 million copies: "indisputably the most widely read and influential book on the human mind, ever published."[63] He uncovered and manipulated our hungering search for answers to life's problems, heartaches, and challenges.

God gently counters. Knowing His sovereignty answers life's challenges, but we must first *unlearn* garbage, in order to learn. Like Jonah, we must turn loose of what can't work for us to then hunt God's answers. We must *unlearn* — everything from the Garden to today isn't about us. It's all about God, and then we start learning God's sovereignty.

Until you let go of your lesser image of God, this book is useless to you. What you've been taught can't work for you. As God has peace for your storm and rest for your turmoil, why not seize His freedom to *unlearn* in order to learn?

Jesus (the Truth), said, "Know the Truth and be free."[64] He meant know Him as God! Non-Christians think all truth sets us free. It can't, or we'd all be free by now! No, until we unlearn lesser and half-truths and trust Truth-Who-has-a-Name —Jesus — we have no One, and no way to experience God as Bondage Buster. And remember, Jesus as Truth followed God completely, trusting His Father's sovereign design for Jesus' life.

---

[62] Trial Preparation. You can google *Hubbard* and *pathological liar* and find multiple sources.

[63] Both the numbers and the marketing hyperbolic language are suspect.

[64] John 8:32.

I want you to see Me

Every Biblical story has people, but the Protagonist, the main character, the Hero is always, always God. Biblical people stories are about God, and He perfects the people.

That seems inescapably simple. How could anyone escape understanding that if they read the Bible, worshipped God, and served Jesus? We do miss it.

Tom: let me use a story in the Bible to frame my story.

In an astounding story of one man against a nation, Elijah, God's prophet stands alone surrounded by a nation to confront 450 prophets for an idol, Baal. The queen supports their idol. Most of the nation slip into Baal worship and two-facedly worship God on Sabbaths. Elijah called thousands of people between two mountains. He signaled a showdown with the false prophets, but first he drew a line in the sand; saying. "How long will you go limping between two different opinions? If the Lord is God, follow Him; but if Baal, then follow him." No one answered him.[65]

How long did I limp or try and hold two opinions?

I would have been one of the people watching, saying nothing, waiting to see how it all played out, but God was out to change all that. His love simply could not leave me alone. Let me tell my story in the next chapter.

---

[65] 1 Kings 18:21.

SECTION 2

Our stories: How God reveals His Truth in our lives.

*We share our lives in these next chapters.
Learn from Tom's,
our friend David Willets' and
then Gary's stories.*

4
My Two-faced Life

Tom: God grew Moses in the most powerful house of the world's most advanced civilization. Moses lived with amazing examples of man's greatness. He saw law, Pharaoh's power over millions of lives, religion, wealth, art — everything that suggests that man is great, that man is the master of his fate.

God grew me in history's most advanced and prosperous country, attending wealthy schools and churches. Due to technological advances, on a summer vacation as a child, I traveled further in a car than a pharaoh in his lifetime. Living in an unbelievable time, it is easy to think of man as amazing, as great.

God readied to immerse Moses in His sovereignty. He kicked him out of Egypt, put him on the worlds' backside with an old priest in a houseful of women, and when the time was ripe — He pushed Moses even further into the wilderness with no witnesses but sheep; to address Moses in a burning bush.

God gave me a cigar smoking lawyer: a frighteningly honest lawyer.

Bob Baxter invited me to his gorgeous ranch near Wetumka in southeast Oklahoma. Oaks and a mixed herd of Herefords and Angus dotted the rolling hills. He welcomed me at the door to his sprawling, limestone ranch house to stay again in the two story guest wing. Bob wanted me to meet a lawyer friend desiring to write a book. I arrived for dinner, Angus beef grilled to perfection, after which we piled into Bob's pickup to ride up to a long deserted cabin

I want you to see Me

where Gene Autry spent summers as a boy, down in "the Indian nation." It is wild to ride into history in the setting sun in a pickup.

At dinner Bob had guided my intro to Gary. I have met charismatic and powerful men all my life, and Gary fit the role. He's gracious, a keen listener, confident and communicates the fearless poise of a man who has lived some of life's tough passages.

Late that night, on the porch we got down to business. Usually, to write a book that means a polite conversation, where I get to know someone to better tell his story.

With the lawyer, Gary Richardson, conversation was more of a full contact sport. Somewhere a little before midnight, he launched into how he found God's sovereignty in a small conference on predestination.

He hit a nerve. Ever since I studied John Calvin in church history at college and seminary, I've known Calvinists and their TULIP[66] — and how they persecuted Anabaptists: my crew. I was not impressed with a brand of Christianity where if they held power, they were repressive and abusive.

I kept an open mind toward Calvin, and came to respect *him*. He was consistent: did you know he was an astrologer? In his day, astronomy was not separate from astrology, and as Calvin believed God ordered the heavens, he also trusted God to speak through them as He did to the wise men, who then sought Jesus. Calvin searched the stars to see what God might reveal. He was consistent in his beliefs.

However, Calvin's followers and formulators alternately bored and bothered me. These formula worshipping people spout a lot about God's greatness, but few live in His sovereign greatness. As a college minister, and later as a pastor, every semester I expected one or two student formulators coming to interview me to see if they

---

[66] TULIP is an acrostic.

My Two-faced Life

wanted to be part of our ministry. Mostly they wanted to know if I was a Calvinist, to walk me through the TULIP acrostic to see how I scored. They notched their theological guns and took measure of the preachers in town.

After a few years, as interviews began, I asked if they were Calvinists. When they enthusiastically said, "Yes!" I then told them I would flunk the interview and suggested a couple of pastors in town where they might find sanctuary and thrive.

So now I leaned on a bannister under bright stars in an immense vault on Bob's porch, looking down on a dark lake reflecting stars' light and discussing predestination with this lawyer. If this were all the prospects his book had, his book felt boring and bothersome. It proved to be anything but boring. It may bother you deeply. It did me.

At one point, Gary even taunted me with, "Can you even tell me one place in scripture where it teaches what you say about man's freedom or God's responding to man's initiatives?" I thought of the places where the Bible says God "relented, repented or changed His mind," but if this lawyer was any good, and it turns out he was exceptional, he would know what any good Calvinist knows to say: "God knew what He was going to do all along, and he was just testing Adam, Abraham, Moses; all of them." I had heard the dodges.

In fact, I had wrestled with and argued on these points with friends for years. As a result, some asked me to stand in their universities and do apologetics in groups of up to 3,000. Some people thought I was good at this. Worse, I thought so. Pride wears amazingly spiritual fashions.

I sized up Gary, drinking wine and smoking a cigar, which made me grateful to be outside, and I wondered what drove him. I asked. He knew the world needed another book on Calvinism like we all need warts.

Something else excited him.

I want you to see Me

He was testing me to see how I handled things. Something else drove Gary. I wanted to see how he handled disagreement. I disagreed with everything he said. He was artful, intelligent, unruffled, and doggedly persistent. Whatever drove him was terribly important to him. In a way, a good theological discussion is like reliving a great chess match or an on-the-edge-of-your-seat Super Bowl game between the Steelers and any opponent. It goes back and forth as opponents reach deeper and pull out what it takes to play better. I wondered what Gary would pull out when he reached deep within.

I didn't squirm or think, "Wow! His take on God's sovereign will is something new!" That does not mean that I didn't miss things. I could easily have been unaware as the topic of predestination dulled my thinking.

Personally, where was I? It's hard to pin down. God's sovereignty was a topic in Systematic Theology along with man's freedom, heaven and hell, soteriology, end times, and so on. God and His sovereignty *were part of a list*, a menu of needed topics for a well-rounded biblical scholar. In church history, Calvin, the TULIP and the Institutes were taught alongside the Roman Catholic humanists, Luther and Zwingli, the Westminster Confession. Again, nothing said, "Among all of these items on the test for Reformation History — *this* is central to all else in your faith in God."

Gary and I discussed one point — a new appreciation of God's sovereignty — that to me got lost among an exploding array of ways that Reformation leaders were wrestling with God's Word and bringing what it said to people.

What I am trying to convey, and may fail to do so — is that God's sovereignty was there all along. It was there all along for Tom in seminary, buried with the rest of history.

God was manifesting Himself to me all along and I missed it. Around Gary, God would open up a multipronged attack on my pride, my intellect, and finally — my heart. The night whispered

My Two-faced Life

God was talking to me this evening through whatever was important, whatever drove this man.

Hours later, I voted to turn in. I thought Gary could nurse that cigar to sunup. Somewhere in the last hour, Gary finally opened up on the book's gist. It would require my sifting through mountains of email between Gary and other people to distill a book, but he had found a foundational piece of God's plan.

Gary was convinced God had no Plan B in Eden's Garden. What God intended was what went down. He is never thwarted. Never put off. Never overridden. God was completely sovereign in Eden.

I was intrigued, if not sold. It constituted another way to understand God's sovereignty, a way new to me. The following morning Gary offered me the job of ghostwriting, and over the next few weeks the task of proving the case from scripture. Gary would not let me write if I did not trust God's sovereignty. That bought another four months of wrangling. In many emails, phone discussions, and visits, he stressed often that I didn't have to agree with the message, but before I wrote with him, I needed to embrace it.

Remember the part about conversation being a full contact sport with Gary? I had to embrace a message: God was sovereign and unthwarted in the Garden of Eden. Everything went down according to God's plan.

Months later, I drove to Tulsa, to meet Gary at Lanna's real estate firm, in her gorgeously appointed conference room to say, "Gary, I am 100 percent on board. God is using this and other things to change my life."

And it stopped there. Garden. God's commitment to us in Jeremiah 29:11 and Philippians 1:6. All of it is great. And all of it was *out there* in time, in the universe, in the world at large: it wasn't in my bed, my checkbook, and my doctor appointments as God intends. As God relentlessly intends.

I want you to see Me

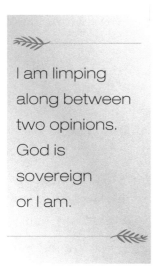

> I am limping along between two opinions. God is sovereign or I am.

You see, we can all do something simple. Silly, but simple. If I am limping along between two opinions — God is sovereign or I am — I can *make progress* by limping closer to God's side. Elijah and Gary and a host of fire-breathers have been saying to people like me for centuries, God doesn't want you 87.3 percent convinced and limping *closer* to His sovereignty.

God's will is that you and I, with all abandon, trust His sovereign will and relax in that. Live it out. Adventure in it. See what it looks like to mature in it. But I get ahead of myself. I thought limping closer to God's sovereignty was a victory. God has a far more black and white definition of victory.

God's painstaking care, His unfathomable patience stuns me. I bought His sovereign hand in Eden as I helped write *Thank God They Ate the Apple!*, but like the Japanese defending Iwo Jima after Americans took the beaches, I did not yield or capitulate anything else. God had to take, to seize hold of every inch of my thinking. It was almost as if I said alongside the Japanese on Iwo Jima, "Okay, God. You are sovereign on the beaches, but can You be sovereign in the mountains?" How many billions of times has God done this exact conversation? Here is one.

God[67] patiently taught an idiot, a wicked king named Ahab, (married the original Jezebel) that He is sovereign. Kings (and writers like me!) have a hard time grasping God's greatness. Simultaneously, God was showing Ahab's enemy, the king of Syria, Benhadad, that He was sovereign as well.

God sent an old prophet to Ahab predicting God would deliver Ahab against Benhadad and 32 other kings using nothing but Ahab's

---

[67] 1 Kings 20:23-27.

My Two-faced Life

bodyguards. Ahab sent the bodyguards, he just sent 7,000 soldiers behind them. Give him a shred of credit; he sent the bodyguards out front. Do you see how we obey *and* cover God's bets? When we cover His bets we tell Him, "You're sovereign in many places, but this place, this time is new, so I'll play it safe."

Translated, "I refuse to give you this part of my life. In spite of all You've proven in other areas of my life, *this area* is new for me to trust You."

God won Ahab a victory, and the prophet predicting the victory promised Ahab: Benhadad was returning for a rematch next spring. Why? His counselors advised Benhadad, "Israel's gods are mountain gods. We fought Israel's army in the hills — that's why they defeated us. But if we fight them on flat land, there's no way we can lose."

How silly of them! How silly for me. Is it the same sort of silly for you? God proved Himself **here** and **there**, but now my concern, my personal battle is **over there**! Now I fear **this**. Now I'm anxious about **this** mess!

God paid for me to research His sovereignty in the Garden of Eden. I didn't translate that sovereignty as true over the thousands of years since, or eternity before, yet.

That opens an important question. How readily do you apply something new God shows you in one part of your life into other areas of your life? Let me ask it another way. If God demonstrates He is sovereign over your marriage, how soon do you then seek Him as sovereign over your finances? How soon do you then seek His sovereignty over your life choices?

As you will read, Gary walked through terrible times in his life. He went to the Word, desperate for answers as to how God could be sovereign after he had lived the life he had lived. I on the other hand, tended to get stuck in what I knew of the Word and stuck in ruts of how to interpret His Word. I missed deep errors in how I

69

I want you to see Me

had lived my life serving God only to find out I tried to *manage* God in the very way(s) I served Him.

At key points in my life, I clung to security as an idol. As others left the comfort of serving in established churches to build from a garage or living room what God chose them to build, I always chose a more secure way to serve — an established church. I won't second guess God. I'm not wondering if I had another life path. Let the songwriters and script writers who do not know God crank out that silliness. He directed my steps.

But, as God has demonstrated His sovereignty over and over to me, I have to now look at my decision to go and serve Him anywhere with new questions. Consider these questions as a way to better help you hear God lead you.

1. For whose glory am I doing this? God's or mine? When younger, I took speaking engagements to large gatherings without blinking. I prayed as the time got closer, but I figured God would be glorified as I spoke in larger places. The glory thing goes to the heart of that first commandment. God isn't out to share His glory.

2. When I speak, whose honor do I speak of first and foremost? You may, like me, think that is a no brainer, so let me show you subtle ways that we fool ourselves. Who is the Hero in your stories about God? God or you? I teach students now to tell their story in Christ and count the pronouns in their testimony. If there are more first person pronouns (I, mine, me) than third (He, His, Him) your story may be confusing to other people as to who gets the honor. See it another way. Do you gloss over places and times when you were helpless? If God used Gary to point a glaring spotlight on my life, it was here. It was second nature for me to tell all about God — without casting much light on my failings, foibles — when I was completely helpless.

My Two-faced Life

3. Another tough test for God's sovereign glory is how faceless can you be? Can you tithe and on top of your tithe then give so quietly that you have to make an intentional point to teach those disciplines to your children? How many people have you helped in life so silently, so surreptitiously that it is God to Whom they give credit?

4. This one came "sideways" to me: Who is your Defender? Do you run your own PR company, always promoting you and never exposing your weaknesses? When my wife read Gary's story, she stumbled where Gary did indefensible things and — did not defend himself in print. I had done things to hurt people in my flock. Indefensible. Not even a great defense lawyer could get me off for being thoughtless and far worse — intentionally hurting other brothers or sisters in Christ.

As we worked together, Gary didn't hide anything. He put his life out there as it was. That made it easy to write. When you and I stand before the sovereign God as Judge over our lives, He will be fully glorious, worthy of all honor, all credit, and Jesus will be my only Defender. What a glorious privilege to be able to live in accord with all of that today, now, here. I don't wear two faces with my Defender. Why did I to wear two faces with Sovereign God?

I had to post one more change in my thinking. Gary wasn't trying to convince me of anything. God was.

And God was speaking through others as well. When Gary and I met, he was through his process to understand God's sovereign glory. Like all of us, he is still working out how to live it, but heart and soul, Gary was on board the night we first talked under the stars.

Mentally, that moved him to another category for me. For some reason, it is always a little more credible for me if I watch you make the transition, make a change, adopt a new position.

You see, God had shown His sovereignty to me through teachers and preachers, but it was as if I wore too-dark sunglasses. Even as a

I want you to see Me

young boy, I listened to presidents of the Southern Baptist Convention, Sidlow Baxter of Oxford, Eddie Lieberman, and both Angel and Homer Martinez. As I surrendered to preach and attended college and seminary God let me sit under Rowena Strickland, first woman Ph.D. from Southwestern Baptist Seminary, Drs. Yandall Woodfin, "Cactus Jack" MacGorman, James Timberlake, William Hendricks, and a host of others. Wise men and women, who all loved God, held scripture as unalloyed truth, and lived lives yielded to Him. From them, I heard our overawing God's sovereignty in a symphony, rather than the builder of the concert hall. Sovereignty was in the music, but not necessarily the Benefactor for the symphony, and the Composer and the Conductor.

Essentially, my mentors pushed me into the world serving an all-powerful God Who had saved me and gave me great freedom at a great price. My job — was to balance freedom (mine) and sovereignty (His).

It was easy. I had two things to keep me stuck in my thinking: our music and our language. Two-faced people look for things coming in twos.

Our music

Some scholars think we get as much as 65 percent of our theology from hymns: our music. My hymns celebrated salvation, walking with God, serving the Master, and being like Jesus — but praising God, adoring His majesty, glorying in His greatness — we did that in the first ten hymns in a hymnal containing 550 songs.

Much like the other 540 hymns in our song book, the rest of my life in Christ felt like it was up to — me. God would *go with* me in my life — which confused me. How could He *go with* me if God was everywhere? God would *lead* me, *bless* me, and help me stay *close* to Him. Our songs taught me to love God, knowing He wanted to *help* me live for Him.

In Sunday school (my grandmother stood outside the delivery room and enrolled me at the age of one scream) we studied the Bible's men and women who loved God. We teach their stories to remember the people, as if the stories are about the people, rather than God. My teachers did a theological two-step (awkward as Baptists can't dance) as they skirted the issue of God's sovereignty — by stressing our responsibilities as believers, and how we *let* God use us. I was told to be *committed*, be *active* at church, and *choose to serve God first*.

The music, the hymns and worship weren't bad just incomplete. I left thinking it was all about me, and I could trust God to do His part.

Over the years, I have watched an explosion of worship songs all showing our hunger for God's greatness, His sovereign goodness and mercy — and Will. Those writers and singers felt the void I felt.

Our language

Then there was our language — especially in revivals, and we had five a year: I mean week-long revivals where each service ended with us singing decision hymns imploring people to come to Christ for twenty minutes or longer. And then, people *accepted* Jesus as personal Savior. I was confused: who was accepting whom? God came and lived the perfect life and died a horrible death — who were *we* to accept *Him*? We could also rededicate our lives and even get saved again and re-baptized if the intervening life was depraved enough.[68] Moreover: once we got saved what was there for God to do?

---

[68] Gary and I grew up in two denominations that stress our (man's) part in salvation. In his Nazarene denomination, if you sinned, you were lost again. As a Baptist, we trusted God's sovereignty enough so that if we were saved, we were saved forever. I know, you are laughing at us because we Baptists keep enough sovereignty for fire insurance, and not much else.

I want you to see Me

It all depended on God for the saving part, but on us and God in some mystical, safety net way, for ***staying in*** or ***staying close***. We *let God* lead us, help us, and hold us in Him. If you want to see Gary get flushed in the face rise up out of a chair — repeat that last phrase: we *let God* use us. I heard it a thousand times growing up. My church would never have preached Ben Franklin's "God helps those who help themselves;" but we *let go* and *let God* all the time.

But God was faithful. I took campers to a camp where I did not want to be, without my pastor there — but God brought Stuart Briscoe. Stuart minimized the damage I might do as a minister. This pastor wrote Billy Graham's discipleship materials for new believers, and spent the ***entire*** week in Acts' second chapter preaching one sermon with ten different takes: Christ is Lord. We have no other relationship; no other way to know, love, or follow God.

I still cycled in and out on God's sovereignty, but my approach, my relationship was now that He is Lord. He is benign dictator, CEO, president, chief of staff — and He is not running for office. Ever.

I know, you are wondering how close an educated guy can get ***to*** something and still not get it. Two-faced people can limp along for long times.

God began again in me. He readied me to hear Him better. I was a little older than Moses. I was failing as a pastor, so said my Personnel Committee: many of them friends. I took that failure home and let it out as anger, so I was failing as a father and husband.

And my horizon was shrinking. God had always blessed me with friends in many stations of life, states, countries and callings. But for years I pulled into myself, into my little world. I quit initiating or responding to others far away, and this is such an insight into God's character. You see when God had Paul write, "God who foreknew us, predestined us"[69] God chose a precise word for predestined. That Greek word is *prehoridzo*, or *prehorizoned*. God had chosen my

---

[69] Romans 8:29.

My Two-faced Life

horizons for me when He began His good work in me, and now, just like for Moses, God was shrinking my horizons. He let my network cede from me. He let my failures come roost in my heart. He began a process in me and Gary was part of that process, but not the biggest part. God tends to reserve that spot for Himself.

God shrank my horizons more. In 2000, my father grew gravely ill. I flew to Beaumont, TX for his last ten days. In the last two days, all the signs said dad would pass soon, and I knew God held dad's life precious.[70] Finally on my last day home, I had to fly out to get back and preach, my heart ached, and I knew God was sovereign over my dad's life and passing. What to do?

Let me whisper in tears, if you serve a sovereign God Who holds all things in His hands, you'll walk a little taller, and act as if you serve Someone far greater than in your past. I was packed; my bags in mom's car. I stood by my dad knowing I would not see him again in this world. What to do?

I prayed into his ear as my sisters and mom held each other. I claimed God's sovereign presence and glory in dad's passing. I dismissed my dad (as if a soldier) into God's presence. I kissed him, and Mom whisked me off at the last possible minute — and five minutes from the driveway on our way to the airport — dad passed into God's presence.

I claimed it, claimed God's sovereign purpose in the minute — and left five minutes before God moved, confirming His divine purpose. Close again. So close. Months later I was biking before attending a personnel committee meeting I had requested in order to tell them I was a tired and crispy pastor.

Going so fast I could not keep up peddling downhill with the wind at my back, I flipped a bike over into a ditch and landed on my helmet. I fractured five vertebrae, compressed vertebra T7 50 percent and

---

[70] God, unlike me, holds all lives equally, stunningly, amazingly precious. See how many ways God's sovereignty is our hope and salvation?

I want you to see Me

T11 60 percent, fractured ten ribs in fourteen places, deflated both lungs, knocked my kidneys offline, shattered my left ankle and shoved a stalk of something up perfectly against my shin bone where it hid for two years on X-rays and almost killed me with sepsis. And they cut away my favorite pair of bike pants when they didn't have to do so.

I was the only one on that stretch of road, riding with a 30+ mile-an-hour tail wind that suddenly whipped and pushed me off the road hurtling into a ditch.

Nothing but wind.

In the ambulance, on my way to an E.R. (miracles of timing) God whispered, "This is not about your church, your marriage or kids. This is about you."

That night my three attending physicians consulted and disagreed. Two did not think I would make it through the night, and the third thought I would make it: never to walk again. My horizons shrunk to a bed on the fifth floor of Stillwater Medical Center. I could not turn over as I had tubes coming out of both lungs trying to re-inflate them.

I must be hard of hearing, so God put me where I could listen better. Two-faced people are better at talking than hearing. Moses was in a wilderness for forty years cleaning wax out of his ears and heart so he could hear better. Gary spent eleven years in his. God is frighteningly patient.

One night in my hospital room, I encountered the living God in the door between the worlds. The streaming golden light, the glory and splendor of heaven, backlit God as He questioned me. In those seconds, I knew that everything boils down to God and His mercy for me. Nothing else in life matters at the end. Nothing. In that moment — when I knew it is all about God — He left me back here on earth. My doctors were so surprised.

Now my church had a crispy pastor who had been in God's presence and was physically broken as well as spiritually. I sat in my

My Two-faced Life

office one afternoon and wondered if I had failed God or if He was unhappy with my life and service and so He had gone on to bless other folks.

It did not occur to me to ask, "Why should I wait until the end of my life to live like God is everything, is sovereign, is all that matters?" I kept plodding along as if it all depended on me, forgetting that it all depends on Him. Adding injuries to a man already limping between two opinions may not turn the trick.

I would have stared at Elijah screaming, "How long can you limp between two opinions?"[71] I might have fidgeted. My heart may have been pounding in my ears. But I would have left him out there alone arguing for God's sovereignty, while I played it safe in the faceless crowd. I do not claim to be a quick learner. I lived past my 55th birthday.

I always thought I would die before age 55. God laughed and asked me about that on my 56th birthday. I know. How many times must God show me, any of us that He is sovereign? Or, over how many areas of my life can I see God as sovereign, and still ***not know*** that He is sovereign over every area of my life; and all of time; and all the universe?

I read the Bible more and other authors less, and my horizon shrank again! We buried Mom and a man professed Christ as Lord at her funeral. Once more, I knew. God gave us twenty years and one week with mom when we asked for twenty years — at the same time that the best cancer doctors at MD Anderson gave her weeks.

God directed Mom's days, not MD Anderson's best cancer doctors. Those docs came around to credit the "X" factor. Mom laughed and said, "'X,' that's funny! That's how the first letter in Christ's name appears in Greek!" She rarely misses a moment.

I resigned as a pastor. I stepped away from being a professional in religion. My resignation is public record. I told my church, "I

---

[71] 1 Kings 18:21.

I want you to see Me

have begun to think I am in the way of God moving in this body of believers." I thought it was honest. God probably sees it as pure hubris.

I questioned everything about me. Can I suggest that is what I think Jonah did in the stinky fish belly down somewhere below the deep blue Mediterranean for three long days, actually dark, slushy, stinky nights? At least I had a beautiful home and a wife who loves me and walks through all of this craziness with me. How kind He was to give me Jill.

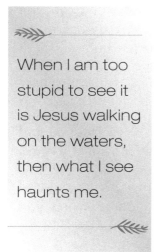

When I am too stupid to see it is Jesus walking on the waters, then what I see haunts me.

I began to reinvent my life, trying to follow what I understood God was doing. Please do not ask what God was doing. I still have a hundred questions and only a hint at some answers. Sorry, if you were hoping for a five-easy-steps-to-understand-sovereign-God's-will-for-your-life. Wrong book. I know we are all to bring Him glory and that gives Him great pleasure.

Thank God They Ate the Apple! had intrigued me, but beyond the Garden of Eden, Gary and I argued and grappled with the Word of God on a hundred topics. I relished the times, as God continued to shrink my horizons and Gary was a great foil, and even better — he was paying me.

Finally, I began to question my balancing act of my two faces — man's freedom and God's sovereignty. Remember, I learned it that way in my university and seminary — a believer strikes a balance between man's freedom and God's sovereignty.

In time, I began writing this book, researching and relearning these stories. All these stories about God in these men and women's lives haunted me. You know how it works. When I am too stupid to see it is Jesus walking on the waters, then what I see haunts me,[72] just

---

[72] Matthew 14:26.

My Two-faced Life

like the disciples in the boat screaming like girls because they thought Jesus was a ghost walking on the waters. Stories meant to encourage me, haunted me.

I found this take away. If God has something to change in you — He kindly sends others to confirm the change. Obviously dad's home going, a near death experience, mom's miraculous extension in life, and Gary's arguments were not enough for me to grasp God's sovereign hold over everything.

Did I say I do not claim to be a quick learner? Fortunately, God has planned a patient, relentless persuasion as my Teacher.

I talked to my brother, Buck who ministers with his wife, Carole, and son, Colt, in prisons in north central New Mexico. People know Buck and his *Big Book* from gun shows to weekly studies in prisons to mission fields. Buck had quietly changed. He grabbed an unyielding hold on God's sovereignty. Buck was the first one I saw changing.

Without asking, I found that my son, Colt, another Oklahoma Baptist University graduate and worship leader with his band and wife, Claire; had rooted deeply in God's sovereign grasp on life. Colt underwent two aortic valve reconstructions. They stopped his heart in two surgeries. Every marathon he runs, he trusts God's sovereign plan for his life. That was two people changing.

Robert and Melanie Krumrey served as our college ministers, and moved their family to plant a church in Amherst, MA. Robert now preached God's sovereign hold over — everything. Imagine flying to Massachusetts and sitting in a car with a pastor, holding that conversation on God's sovereignty — parked in a cold drizzle outside the First Church in Northampton, MA, — Jonathan Edward's church!

See three things in Edwards whose work I read in my thirties.

1. Cognitive scholars believe his IQ was north of 600.

2. It would be hard to find anyone more unshakable in the face of adversity safely abiding in God's sovereign will. Anyone.

I want you to see Me

3. Oh, and ground zero for America's First Great Awakening was that church I saw through a windshield's rain diamonds. Edwards the pastor, read two-hour-long sermons in a high voice as people opened church windows in winter so those outside in snow could hear God's Word. They ached to hear of God's greatness.

Robert and I sat in his truck that night in a cold drizzle, and talked of God's unchanging will, His mercy, His holiness and righteousness. What I had read from Edwards back in my thirties[73] came back to me. Even more funny is that I introduced Robert to Edward's writings. Now the student was teaching his teacher. Now three people had changed on me to find God sovereign when nothing else in theology or life yielded any answers, but others were signaling to me that they unequivocally held to God's sovereignty. Turns out preaching two-faced is like preaching blandly. God moved in so many ways that I would have to have been arguing with Him all the time to have missed all He was showing me. Okay, I was arguing with Him all the time. Except when I was sleeping. Okay, maybe some of my dreams involved arguing about this. . . .

Maybe you argue or whine. Is *life* not working out as you hoped? Are *you* not working out as you hoped? Is God not behaving as you wanted? Is He not janitoring for you? Has He refused to take a hiatus in your life?

May I show you a picture that slowly made sense to me? I have not seen this anywhere, but use it if it helps make sense of God's sovereignty. See three evolving ways I saw the world. Way One. This is how I saw reality in seminary. I divided the universe into God's sovereignty and what He gave to us to steward for Him. You can see my two faces in the two sides.

---

[73] *The Works of Jonathan Edward's Volume 1 & 2.* Banner of Truth 1996.

My Two-faced Life

My first "way" to see the world as a believer

God Gave This to Man	God Kept This for Himself
Science	The Future
Economics	The work of Salvation
Society	The laws of Physics, Creation, Biology
Civilization	
Law	His Kingdom
Sexuality and all of	His Calling
our Personhood	His Divine Purposes beyond my thoughts
Man's free choices	Heaven and His Mystery

In my thinking God *was* sovereign — over in His area, in His place, and He had decided I could be free, translated sovereign, in my place.

Then dad died. I almost died, and I talked to God in the doorway between the worlds. Mom died and as my horizons shrank, God pushed another picture to me. It would take me years to see, but God kept moving parts of my thinking from a "two column" way of seeing the universe, into a "One Column" way of seeing the world.

My second "way" to see the world as a believer

God Gave This to Me	God Holds these in Sovereignty
~~Science~~	Science and the Future
~~Economics~~	The work of Salvation
~~Society~~	Economics, Society, Civilization,
~~Civilization~~	Law, The laws of Physics, Creation,
~~Law~~	Biology, Sexuality, our Personhood
~~Sexuality~~	His Kingdom
~~Man's~~	His Calling, His Divine Purposes beyond
Tom's free choices.	my thoughts
Tom's terrible sins.	Heaven and His Mystery

I want you to see Me

Think of it. My last two pieces to see as completely contained in God's sovereign will and purposes were — my free choices and my terrible sins. I kept seeing my mistakes: obvious, terrible mistakes. Sins I committed against others stayed with me because I will stand and give an account[74] before God at the end of life — every idle word, every idle deed — indeed. I did not need a change in my head. I needed a change in my heart so I could *see* differently. It came, so slowly as I limped away from the lies to finally look like this.

My final way to see God's sovereignty

> **God Holds *all* in sovereignty**
> Science and the Future
> The work of Salvation
> Economics, Society, Civilization, Law,
> The laws of Physics, Creation, Biology
> Sexuality and all of our Personhood
> His Kingdom
> His Calling. My freedom. My choices.
> His Divine Purposes beyond our understanding
> Heaven and His Mystery
>
> EVERYTHING. PERIOD.
>
> *God left this to me:*
> *Be in Him doing His Will.*

All is contained in God's sovereignty. All is unified, and oh, God is into unity. All is within His Will. I leave it to theologians to discuss that. All I have to do is live like that is true.

---

[74] Jesus spoke of this in Matthew 12:36-37. John wrote about this in Revelation 20:12.

My Two-faced Life

And guess what? My heart is in better shape than in the years I pastored. My physician volunteered that to me after my last stress test. Oh, and I only have one face to put on when I go out every day. And the adventure of any given day is more audacious than before. Looking at the world to know God's will and follow it is far, far larger and more demanding than getting up to "freely" figure out, "What do I want to do today?"

Okay, all this sovereignty may be scary, but remember: Jesus' first day on the job as our resurrected Lord scared *every one* of the believers. He had to say to everyone, "Peace" as soon as each person who had known Him before the crucifixion now saw Him gloriously. God, Who is sovereign even over death, had raised His Son from the dead; and instead of raising Jesus straight to Heaven and flushing the earth experiment, Jesus was walking around, arguing the scriptures, eating, telling everyone not to be afraid of Truth. Sovereignty is truer than death, truer than the world's mightiest government (Rome at the time), truer than anything.

So being slightly scared makes sense. It's what you do next that is important. It is how you live now that has Heaven on the edge of its seat, hanging on what God does in you, what He does through you next.

Gary, it turns out, was living my struggle with me. He bent over backwards to be patient and professional, but he ached for me to know what had finally given him release and peace. That marks someone who gets God's sovereignty. The timing grated on Gary's nerves, but he bit his lip to keep from showing it and trusted God's timing.

Gary: "I shuddered to think of the help it might be to so many people if Tom, a preacher with multiple degrees, would just open his life, his struggle, up to readers — what he went thru to get to a place where He trusted God. In the writing process, he related incidents but skipped the struggle. To me, we owe our struggles to a reader who will face his or her struggle."

I want you to see Me

Did Gary despair for me? You judge. He wrote: "I am honestly beginning to wonder what to think. Did you just jack with me and have a strong sovereignty belief all along or do you easily forget? Or don't want to recall? Some things you said to me were completely anti-sovereign. Now, you seem to want to act as if you never said them, never believed that. It baffles me."

In case you thought that my process looked coherent, consistent, or intentional as I limped along, read that again.

James described me well. Think "ouch" as I say "well."

"Whoever doubts is like the surf of the sea, tossed and turned by the wind. People like that should never imagine that they will receive anything from the Lord. They are double-minded, unstable in all their ways."[75]

Gary has this point in his life, [spoiler alert] driving down 71st street in Tulsa, OK when God broke him and tears flowed and Gary knew he had given God his greatest fears and helplessness. If you have that, then thank God. He has been magnanimous to you.

I don't have that point in time. My experience is a more of a huge stroke across time. It is hard for me to know when it started and when it ends. I thought there were times I limped along at 37 percent sovereignty and then 91 percent belief in God's sovereign love for me. I don't think it has ended. It is a mystery to me. There was a time when I wrestled with this. Fought it. Maybe educational degrees slowed me, tripped me, or left me silently trying to hold two opinions for so, so long.

I no longer fight. I only hold one opinion. One face.

C.S. Lewis wrote about this process where God is alongside us and we don't recognize Him and miss His working. Lewis wrote

---

[75] James 1:6-8.

My Two-faced Life

of a young boy named Shasta in *A Horse and His Boy*.[76] Shasta stole a talking horse to escape to a magic land called Narnia where a mythical creature, a Lion reigns. He got there to find the *myth* terrifyingly real. Aslan tells this runaway boy, Shasta, that throughout his adventure on leaving slavery and heading for what turns out to be his destiny, he saw Aslan repeatedly throughout the story. Shasta is stunned.

Aslan tells Shasta he appeared as both cat and lion in differing parts of the adventure. At every turn Aslan (the Christ figure) was with Shasta and the others that joined him, protecting them, guiding them, giving them rest, and cracking a whip if they moved too slowly — even frightening them to get them home in time to warn everyone in this kingdom of an impending invasion. In the conversation, Aslan reveals that He — the Christ figure — is more real, far greater, and far fiercer than the boy had dreamed.

And He is more present than we see. Thus the title of the book. Sovereignty means God is present. He is present to show us He is sovereign.

Think of it. Each disciple changed from loving and following a rabbi named Jesus of Nazareth to bowing down and surrendering his life and death to God's Son! That change was so great that Simon was renamed by Jesus — as Peter. That is all of our stories, and why God brought Gary into my life.

God wanted me to see Him leap from the Bible's pages to vanquish my fears and theology by His Truth. It did not happen all at once for me, like it did for Gary. It came in waves; it nuanced my dogged and blind ways and days trying to serve God, like He needed that. I had to come to the end of myself and know that I needed Him far, far more than He needed me. Actually, He does not need me in the least, and yet, and yet His love has reached to me and will

---

[76]   C. S. Lewis. (1954). *The Horse and His Boy*, Geoffrey Bles, London. Is the fifth book published in Lewis' *Chronicles of Narnia*.

I want you to see Me

not leave me alone, will not leave me unchanged, and refuses not to use me to His glory.

So what is my testimony? Go with Who you know. God had to show me repeatedly Who I knew. Let me point to two things that got (get?) in my way on knowing.

I see in me and my culture a brand of *academiaitis*. We contract *academiaitis* at universities. If I ask, "Do you know accounting?" You may say, "Yes!" But I must press further to have you be clear about whether that means you made a C in Intro to Accounting, or you are a successful CPA. When flying, I don't want a guy sitting in the left side of my jet's cockpit with a lot of head knowledge about planes, weather, and flying. As I buckle up listening to a stewardess give the safety spiel while watching thunderstorms outside, I want to know that the guy flying left side has tens of thousands of hours of doing, of acting, of flying planes and this plane in particular.

I don't want a doctor who read books on surgery replacing my son's aortic valve. No, I want a doctor who performed hundreds of operations, specifically ***this*** operation. My danger is having read, even preached on a topic that I think, "I know this stuff!"

I must let the reality of God's sovereignty wash through me, wash through my marriage, my physical and financial holdings, my relationships, and my ways of conducting business. Like the pilot and doctor, I must continually encounter God in His sovereignty. I must respond to Him as Truth.

I must move beyond book learning and get on with life applying. The wisest souls I know went with what they knew of God's sovereign will, love, mercy, and plan for their lives.

Second, I must breathe in humility in light of God's greatness. My brother, Buck, has told me I need to be humble since I was sixteen. Really!? Yes, sixteen. I used to say, "God said it. I believe it. And that settles it." Now, in increasing humility I whisper, "God said it, and that settles it."

And I trust Him. Children seem to grasp this.

My Two-faced Life

Perhaps adulthood's biggest danger is thinking everything depends on us, so it is all about us. Again, like the children Christ bids us become, we make plans and leave results to Almighty God.[77] That may feel a *little* two-faced to you.

Maybe two-faced is too strong a word for you. It is terrible. So, let's sift through some other words. Diverged, conflicted, clashing, anxious, torn, disputed — powerful words all. Don't they describe a lot of what you see in churches and in God's people? People drive nice cars, live in nice houses and give almost nothing to God? They feel empty, powerless, conflicted, and guilty.

Trying to live as if we could be free from God's sovereignty carries price tags. Consider: mental disorders are common.[78] We know Jesus did not come to heap burdens or bondage on anyone. He came to take our burdens![79] He healed, cleansed and forgave people with all manner of afflictions.

But if you don't trust Jesus and God as sovereign. If you don't believe or live as if God heals or take our burdens, then look only at the mental disorders that describe the above aspects of a divided soul: diverged, conflicted, clashing, anxious, torn, and disputed.

- Over 26 percent of adults[80] suffer[81] from a diagnosable mental disorder in a given year[82] — 57 million people![83]

---

[77] Proverbs 16:9; Isaiah 8:10; Jeremiah 29:11.

[78] http://www.nimh.nih.gov/health/publications/thenumberscountmentaldisordersin America/index.shtml.

[79] Matthew 11:30.

[80] Ages 18 and older.

[81] All figures are for the United States.

[82] Kessler RC, Chiu WT, Demler O, Walters EE. Prevalence, severity, and comorbidity of twelvemonth DSM IV disorders in the National Comorbidity Survey Replication (NCSR). *Archives of General Psychiatry*, 2005 Jun; 62(6):61727.
Kessler RC, Berglund PA, Demler O, Jin R, Walters EE. Lifetime prevalence and age of onset distributions of DSMIV disorders in the National Comorbidity Survey Replication (NCSR). *Archives of General Psychiatry*. 2005 Jun; 62(6):593602.

[83] U.S. Census Bureau Population Estimates by Demographic Characteristics. Table 2: Annual Estimates of the Population by Selected Age Groups and Sex for the United States: April 1, 2000 to July 1, 2004 (NCEST200402) Source: Population Division, U.S. Census Bureau Release Date: June 9, 2005. http://www.census.gov/popest/national/asrh/

I want you to see Me

- Mental disorders are a leading cause of disability.[84]

- Some 20.9 million in a given year, have a mood disorder.[85]

- Major depressive disorder hurts 14.8 million Americans in a given year.[86]

The costs of living as an end to ourselves, as free over God's sovereignty, seem high when seen this way. We can catalogue disorders, but the result is the same. So many people suffer when we push for our freedom over God's sovereignty.

When I am free with no sovereign God to whom I can run, in whom I can trust — my mind and soul weren't made to work healthy without my Creator.

Now, please read David's story. David's story held my heart in a vise the entire time I first heard it. It will grip yours as well.

---

[84] The World Health Organization. *The global burden of disease: 2004 update*, Table A2: Burden of disease in DALYs by cause, sex and income group in WHO regions, estimates for 2004. Geneva, Switzerland: WHO, 2008. http://www.who.int/healthinfo/global_burden_disease/GBD_ report_2004update_AnnexA.pdf.

American Psychiatric Association. *Diagnostic and Statistical Manual on Mental Disorders, fourth edition (DSMIV)*. Washington, DC: American Psychiatric Press, 1994.

[85] Kessler RC, Berglund P, Demler O, Jin R, Koretz D, Merikangas KR, Rush AJ, Walters EE, Wang PS. The epidemiology of major depressive disorder.

[86] Ibid.

5

Our Monolith: God

*"God allows those things He hates
to accomplish those things He loves."*[87]

What is five seconds to you?[88]

One Mississippi, two Mississippi, three Mississippi, four Mississippi, five Mississippi.

You can go out the front door and get to the morning paper in five seconds.

You can stop, put your arm around your spouse and start a great kiss.

You can snap a stunning snapshot as the sun sets.

You can say hello and shake hands with a friend in five seconds.

As the sun drew close to setting on Thursday, March 4, 2004, around seven o'clock in the evening my life was radically altered by an event that took all of 5 seconds from start to finish.

What happened not only reshaped how I now live, but it completely altered the nature of my personal relationships, changed

---

[87] Tada, J. E. (2003). *The God I Love*.
[88] We are indebted to Dr. David Willets for allowing us to walk with him through his life's darkest days. To access great resources that he has for you, especially if you are grieving, go to www.silverlining.ws.

I want you to see Me

the direction of my career path, and transformed my core beliefs concerning God's sovereignty.

Before you can grasp how radical was my metamorphosis, let me put my life in context before those five seconds changed everything.

My father ministered as a Southern Baptist pastor in conservative churches in Kentucky, Georgia and Oklahoma. No, I don't remember much from his sermons, but I always respected, yes, admired how he lived his life. Dad earned a Th.D. degree at Southern Theological Seminary in Louisville, KY, but still practiced a childlike trust in God. In particular, while dad supported my mother through eight years of agonizing cancer induced pain, he never wavered in his belief that God was intimately involved in her whole ordeal — from her diagnosis to her eventual death. They actively prayed for her healing, as did hundreds of others. But God chose to ultimately heal her not by removing the disease from her, but by removing her soul from this earth.

My image of dad was of a man quietly trusting God's plan for his wife, my mother, and all of us touched by her. That was my first, firsthand exposure to how the sovereignty of God functions in a believer's life.

Mom died in 1976. Over the years God has introduced me to dozens of people who were so deeply involved in prayer for mom and our family, that intercessory prayer became the heartbeat of their personal ministries. The Holy Spirit quickened the hearts of others to cry out to God for salvation. Still others facing cancer were encouraged to draw close to the Comforter and Great Physician. Romans 8:28 exploded from a Bible verse to a reality of life in the Kingdom of Sovereign God. God did not waste her life and passing.

I saw God's sovereignty lived out in front of me, but my early theological development had two sides.

Our Monolith: God

Let me back up to being a child and teen. Growing up in a Southern Baptist church meant that I regularly saw the dynamic of an evangelistic invitation. Each year my father regularly scheduled at least two revival meetings. He brought in evangelists, professionals, who typically had bigger than life personalities and delivered booming sermons, great stories, and just enough hellfire to lick at any apathy.

I also literally sweated through evangelistic sermons as a teen at a sprawling camp, Falls Creek, for a week every summer. There great Southern Baptist Convention (SBC) pastors preached as well as evangelists. Frankly, I don't remember much of what was preached, but I vividly remember feeling a heavy, a troubling sense of personal responsibility to *allow God* to do this or that in my life. Everything revolved around my willingness to *let God* come into my heart, to *let God* take control of me, to *let God* make me into the person He wanted me to be.

Don't miss the fact, it was *my will* that was the go or no go crux.

I had this image — God was always standing outside the next door of my life knocking as if He had to ask permission before He could go a little deeper into the abode of this child's life. What power and control we were taught that we have over God!

Of course no one actually taught that. Our teachers knew better than to say such a thing aloud, but it seemed that way, and this fuzzy and vague theology carried powerful effects into my life. Year after year my impressionable mind was pulled between two theologies. One said, "If it's going to be, it's up to me!" and the other said, "God is in control of everything. He is sovereign."

I graduated high school and moved to Shawnee to attend Oklahoma Baptist University. Having loved seeing evangelists in action, I traveled in the summers following my freshman and sophomore years with two friends: we were all named David. It was during a revival meeting at the First Baptist Church of Georgetown, TX, that God exposed a chink in my untested theology.

I want you to see Me

My other teammates both hailed from strong free-will church backgrounds: Nazarene and Assembly of God. We worked well together with my Southern Baptist upbringing, because I was preaching and living on the "let go and let God" side of the SBC. What we lacked in wisdom, we more than compensated for in youthful enthusiasm.

That hot Texas evening after the service, a teammate convinced me that the reason God wasn't healing my mother from cancer was due to either some unconfessed sin or her lack of faith that God would heal her. With the theological discernment of a three-year-old I called my mother and solemnly conveyed this newfound cure for the cancer ravaging her body.

My mother: so godly, so humble — spent her married life walking faithfully beside her pastor husband, enjoying little to no recognition for the continual sacrifices she silently made to advance the Gospel through the local church. Emboldened with brilliant self-righteousness I called her. She endured this painful conversation as my father silently listened on the other phone: "Mom, the reason you aren't being healed is that there must be some sin you haven't confessed. Are you sure you've confessed all your sin to God?"

"Well, David, I don't know. I pray every day for a long time. I'll ask God to reveal anything in my life that isn't pleasing to Him."

"Okay. It could also be that God is not healing you because you just don't have enough faith that He can or will heal you. Mom — do you really believe He can heal you?"

"Son, I truly believe God can do anything. If He wants to heal me He can."

"Well, mom, He wants to heal you because it says in the Bible that He wants to do that. So, it must be an unconfessed sin or your lack of faith."

Dad quietly interrupted, "Lois, do you mind if I talk to David alone for a minute?"

Our Monolith: God

Mom, "I love you son. Goodbye."

Dad, "Son, you know who you sound like to me? Job's three friends. God has all power and authority to heal your mother. If that is His plan for her life, He will heal her. I'd suggest you think through what you say before you say it."

I could only hold an uncomfortable silence lasting several seconds, "Okay, dad," and hang up.

The team finished preaching and singing at the churches that summer. Back at school, I received a phone call from a Tulsa based evangelist I had grown to respect and idolize: Sam Cathy. Sam had taken me under his wing my senior year in high school. He saw some potential in me, or feared such as his daughter and I became acquainted at OBU! Sam was preaching a revival at the First Southern Baptist Church of Del City, OK, and he asked if we could meet for dinner after one of the services. I was honored and delighted!

At dinner, Sam shared his deep concern over my involvement in the doctrines of works salvation and faith healing. He didn't slam charismatic people, he sternly corrected my theology. Sam holds unconditionally to God's unconditional sovereignty, which empowers his serving as an effective evangelist used by God to reveal the elect. Chastened, I listened and began to heed his counsel.

God sowed a new message into my life and ministry. Shortly after our dinner, I ended my partnership with the evangelism team. Did this truth transform me or my message? Some. I graduated OBU, married the most beautiful girl on campus, Leesa Laney, and graduated from Southern Baptist Seminary in 1984.

I then began my first pastorate in fast-growing south Tulsa. Before coming to Parkview Baptist I had served on church staffs at First Southern Baptist, Del City, with Bailey Smith; Immanuel Baptist, Shawnee, with Larry Adams; FBC OKC, with Gene Garrison; and Calvary Baptist in Lexington, KY, with Dan Cooper.

I want you to see Me

All these men taught me vital aspects of effective ministry. I thank God for them.

I knew God had placed in me a pastor's heart, not a vocational evangelist's. Along with that heart God brought hurting people. As Parkview grew into a predominately upper middle class family of execs and entrepreneurs, we also grew in human pain.

- In '86 as national news ran stories of people contracting AIDS, I conducted a man's funeral that died of the little known virus.

- I conducted the funerals of children, victims of suicide and ravenous diseases like cancer and others' untimely deaths.

- People paraded through my life for counseling in the pain of infidelity, business failure, disturbing abuse and seemingly every other challenge facing humanity.

> This was no longer seminary. This was the real world. I needed an articulate answer — for me — before those I served as pastor.

What started as a whisper in my soul rose to a shout, "God, what's the answer to all this pain, suffering and dysfunction?" This was no longer seminary. This was the real world. I needed an articulate answer for me — before the people I served as pastor.

So, I put one together.

I've heard a spiritual genius communicates a theological concept in a pamphlet, not a multi-volume work. That's not totally accurate, but today's preaching pastor is wiser to lean toward a pamphlet before exceeding his listeners' attention span.

Each year I preached a sermon titled something like, "What is God's Will for My Life?" Of course, that question assumes something — that a believer can miss God's will or be out of God's will. My message's bare bones were not untrue: study God's Word, pray, seek the counsel of godly people, listen to the Holy Spirit's voice and try to discern your circumstances. All solid teaching.

But the sermon's unbiblical essence is ***the*** question. In fact the sermon's title should have read; "What is god's will for MY life?" At the core of the message is ME. I said god's kingdom depends on ME to search for god's (small "g") workable will in MY life as he (small "h") sits passively by until **I** (capital "I" in bold) declare a path on which **I** find peace. Worse, this theology insinuates that God is terribly removed from my life until I conclude that he *may* now be active. For you who sat under this teaching for years, please forgive me. I was trying to help, but my "biblical" thinking missed the mark.

But wait. I had another annual sermon! In one form or other, I asked, "Is There an Answer to Evil, Pain and Suffering?" This one was trickier. Here is how the message played out.

- God created the world to be perfect and blissful.

- He gave Adam and Eve everything they needed to thrive and there was no heartache, pain, suffering or death.

- That's how God intended the world to be, not how it turned out to be.

- Here my theology *functionally* treated God much like Plato and Aristotle – God is the First Cause [First Mover]. Once He set the laws of the universe in place, those laws rule the daily affairs of mankind. God is not directly involved in anyone's life.

Now, I would never have dared say I believed this, but *the way* I taught could easily lead one to conclude that I believed this. Back to my sermon; the one I used to preach —

"God placed two trees in the middle of the Garden of Eden – the Tree of Life and the Tree of the Knowledge of Good and Evil. God

I want you to see Me

gave Adam and Eve a choice: free will. If you eat of The Tree of the Knowledge of Good and Evil you bring sin into the world. Along with sin comes all forms of evil, pain, suffering and death."

So, my answer to the problems of evil, pain, suffering and death was that "man (continually) brings those things here because he (we) choose to bring sin into the world. The Hebrews muddled through life keeping the Law of Moses. Israel's plight was simply sin's consequences. God was active in the world only to the extent that He punished wrong, rewarded right, kept His promises and performed the occasional miracle."

Only it is not true. God is more.

But what I used to preach continued; "Through God's infinite love and mercy, Jesus died on a cross to pay the price for the sin that separates sinful man from Holy God. While this earth is stuck in — not released from evil, pain, suffering and death — Jesus places us back in the Garden of Eden *spiritually*." And the sermon's capstone; "It is our choice whether or not we 'accept' or 'receive' Jesus as Lord and Savior. Individuals decide if they want to spend eternity in heaven or hell."

Painfully revisiting this sermon, I thought I was a faithful soldier of the cross and defender of (excuser for) Holy God. But this theology had very little to do with God and everything to do with individual, upper middleclass, North Americans (and Europeans).

The years ticked by to usher in those five seconds.

My lovely Leesa, wife of 27 years, had driven our beautiful high school senior, Lauryn, to OBU to see the campus and was now headed north on the Indian Nations Turnpike in an Oklahoma spring thunderstorm.

One Mississippi: their car hydroplaned, skidding sideways into oncoming traffic. Three Mississippi: a car traveling in that oncoming lane slammed into them. Five Mississippi: killing them both. Probably shorter than the time it took you to read that sentence,

Our Monolith: God

God changed my path in this life. And make no mistake, He planned this event before my wife, daughter and I were even born.

And all of my brilliant theology? It was no help for this descent, this free fall weighing down my heart.

Hours later, my doorbell rang, and I wondered, "Who's at my door on a Thursday night?" I opened to see two uniformed Louisiana Highway Patrolmen. I thought they were there for me as pastor — not as husband, not as father — but they somberly conveyed dry facts. Could they be wrong? No. A cold gripped my heart. Gone. The funerals and memorial services unfolded like a horror movie you can't stop; and dear friends and family tried to say what might help; and then drifted back to their lives; and I, alone, three weeks later entered my house after a few fruitless hours in my office.

The lead line from a popular evangelistic tract, *The Four Spiritual Laws*, reads, "God loves you and has a wonderful plan for your life." I believed that before the five second event — and I believe it now. But God's "wonderful plan for my life" included this painful descent into emotional hell. And in that barren place of emotional torture; I met Sovereign God.

Existing, grieving at that level of pain for the weeks following the car wreck pounded a physical toll on me.

Tiredly I trudged into the house. The silence was palpable. On a thousand other nights, my wife and daughter were there when I came home from work. Their happy greetings and laughter echoed in the pressing, empty stillness.

I now know the meaning of the phrase "dead quiet."

That evening I slowly shuffled to the master bedroom, weeping so bitterly that I almost didn't recognize myself as I walked past a mirror. Once in the bedroom I collapsed. On my knees. My heart shattered. The thought of never seeing them again on this earth was so brutally final. My wife was the love of my youth, and my daughter was the apple of my eye. Both gone. So suddenly, so abruptly.

I want you to see Me

At that moment I turned my face toward heaven to cry out over and over, "You've put too much on me! You've put too much on me!" Where was God in this agony? Where was the Lover of my soul, my Redeemer? Again, I cried out, "If You don't show up in this room, I am going to despair." I did not think to take my own life, although I can no longer judge another person who takes that action in a moment like that. I had it more in my heart to simply curl up into an emotional ball and slowly walk away from God. But God did show up. One Mississippi.

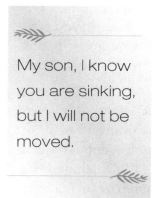

My son, I know you are sinking, but I will not be moved.

He showed not as the *paraklete* (Greek for "One who walks alongside"), nor the Comforter, nor "Papa" (Jesus' endearing name for God). In my mind's eye God arose before me like a gigantic, granite monolith; strong and unshakably solid. Three Mississippi. His presence overwhelmed me! And I heard God say, "My son, I know you are sinking; but I will not be moved."

Five Mississippi. Five seconds. Again.

I understood Isaiah as he watched God's heavenly train fill the sky.[89] I felt like Job when God came to him after querying the Almighty. What happened to me is that the great I Am came as if to say, "Take your eyes off the sinking sand around you. Now, fix them on Me! Keep them on Me! I will not be moved."

Rising to my feet God put Job's prayer in my mind. I confessed to Him, *"Even though you slay me, yet will I trust in You."*[90]

The emotional freefall ensnaring me fell away. Sovereign God came to me. With my eyes fixed on Him I saw that the wreck that took my wife and daughter was no causeandeffect misfortune brought on by the fall of sinful man in the Garden of Eden. This

---

[89] Isaiah 6:1, during the painful loss of the king that Isaiah loved.
[90] Job 13:15, after he sees God and surrenders to His complete sovereignty.

Our Monolith: God

was God's doing. He caused this. His fingerprints were all over it. And He did it all because He loved Leesa, and He loved Lauryn, and He loved my son Landon, and He loved me and wanted to give me a gift that could come to me no other way.

God did not leave those five seconds on an Oklahoma Turnpike unanswered. He gave me five more seconds.

Years have passed, as we write my story. God continually directs my unwrapping this gift. He jack-hammered large chunks of unhealthy ego out of me. With surgical precision God continues to cut away idols from my heart that I fail to realize have taken up residence in there. Like a tapestry of cosmic proportions I have begun to see how God is weaving this event into the fabric of hundreds of people's lives. Everything I had wrapped in my image of serving God: ministry style, size, location and application have been unwrapped and altered to new ones.[91]

My wife of eight years, Melanie, and my son, Landon, continue as beautiful examples of God's kindnesses to me. And another rich blessing to me is Gary. I began my journey to embrace God's sovereignty after the car wreck, but I did not fully do so until a few years later through Gary's mentoring.

Joni Erickson Tada, whose life was drastically altered by a diving accident, says, "God allows those things He hates to accomplish those things He loves."[92] Only a sovereign monolithic, unshakable God, without qualification, can be so faithful and true to love us that much.

> Only a sovereign monolithic, unshakable God, without qualification, can faithfully and truly love us that much.

---

[91] This is Tom. Please visit www.silverlining.ws on the web. See how God uses David and his story today.
[92] Tada, J. E. (2003). *The God I Love.*

I want you to see Me

He completes us as He promises.

Fix your eyes on the God Who delivers on His promises.

6

God's Desert(s) and Finishing School[93]

"It is not that God is the spectator and sharer of our present life . . . but rather that we are the reverent listeners and participants in God's action in the sacred story, the history of the Christ on earth."
—Dietrich Bonhoeffer[94]

Deserts and other God gifts

Ever sweated in a group on a hot day in an old building listening to a tour guide drone on and on about the building? In that hot, dreary speech did you yearn for something truer, deeper than the guide's droning words? Did you hunger for a great historian to paint the people and actions building history in that building? We feel that way during many lectures on sovereignty and knowing God.

You know who God is. We got Him as kids. But do you sense the beautiful things God is doing in you now? Have you missed enjoying Him, understanding how He's working in you?

---

[93] This is Gary's life story as God brought him to see His sovereignty.
[94] Bonhoeffer, D. (1936). *Life Together: the Classic Exploration of Faith in Community*. Augsburger.

I want you to see Me

Where would you go to hear His voice? Would you be in a quiet garden, a still place? Would you seek out a golden sunset beach or a mountain top with air so clean you can see forever?

This chapter visits no gardens, no sunsets and no mountaintops.

In fact, Gary shares his most dry, frightening — and then wonderful — "desert experience." We show how God uses a desert in us. What would you give in your dry, dark place to have a hope, a security that God is using *even your desert* to perfect something wonderful in you?

So — you have no interest to be in a desert. Neither did Gary. In fact, you probably work to avoid deserts.

But what if we can't know God's depths without desert time?[95] What if only spiritual midgets seek to avoid deserts? What if we whispered that when we desire God "like a deer pants for water:"[96] that deer the Psalmist writes about was — you guessed it — in a desert. Please learn what a desert experience is and what it does in us, why its pain is important, why its loneliness is key. Deserts let us glimpse God's sovereignty.

You need a desert. Like a prairie uses fire to cleanse itself and renew its growth, you need a desert. As a forest needs fire periodically to clean out the forest floor and spur new seedlings to grow, you need a desert.

The word "desert" itself is not what you think. Crusaders returning from the arid Middle East in the 13th century coined a word to describe desolate, wild places they had seen: *desert*. These deserts, wild places, these alien wildernesses were so strange to crusading Europeans, yet were home to Arab and Jew, to Persian and Turk. *Desert* has always been in the blood of God's chosen leaders, prophets and preachers.

---

[95] Moses, David, Amos, John the Baptist, Jesus, Paul to name a few all spent extensive time in the desert.

[96] Psalm 42:1 A psalm of David.

God's Desert(s) and Finishing School

But! The word desert, oddly enough, has *nothing* to do with sand or dryness. It means "to separate." So God takes us into deserts to separate us — from things.

It may be obvious, but in deserts God separates us from *things*. What may not be obvious are the things God separates from us, or *why* He separates us from those things.

Going under a surgeon's knife for cancer surgery, I trust her to know which tissues will kill me, and which I need to live. A surgeon into whose hands I literally put my life will cut, *will separate from me* killing tissues. I trust **why** she cuts out cells including some healthy tissue that is embroiled in the cancer.

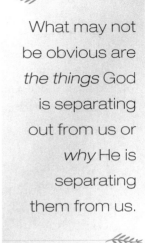

What may not be obvious are *the things* God is separating out from us or *why* He is separating them from us.

It is the same as God separates **things** from me in my desert. I may feel some things are not bad at all: profession, houses/land, money, even relationships and sometimes — family. I can elevate anything before Him. But if cancer cells ensnare these things, God may remove them just as a surgeon might to save my life.

God, who truly, profoundly loves us,[97] knows what brings us life and what brings us death.[98]

So, as God shapes a desert's beauty by separating water from the landscape, He likewise separates our good ideas from poor or deathly ideas. Sometimes gently, and sometimes like a tornado, He blows away lies and notions we use as crutches.

We see *bad* things in friends' lives — terrible relationships or addictions that are killing them. It is harder to see *good* things in us,

---

[97] Romans 5:8. But God shows His love for us, because while we were still sinners Christ died for us.

[98] Exodus 20:46. In the Song of Solomon, God says He loves us as a king loves His new Bride (4:9, 10). In the book of Revelation 19:7 and 21:2 we are Christ's Bride at the end of time.

103

I want you to see Me

things like food, sex and entertainments that are out of balance and twisting us and draining us of love or life.

> **Desert:** noun \de zrt\
>
> 1 arid land with sparse vegetation; especially: such land having a very warm climate and receiving less than 10 inches of sporadic rainfall annually.
>
> 2 archaic: a wild, uninhabited tract
>
> 3 a desolate or forbidding area lost in a desert of doubt
>
> **Origin** Latin, *desertum*, from *de* + *serere* to join together. ~ 13th century

Exactly here, in a desert's heat, God sears away half or twisted truths keeping us from seeing Christ as *the* Truth. He separates out killing things. The almost truths, like mirages, are illusions promising what they can't deliver.

In a desert God ultimately separates us from the final, most deadly illusion: that anything — *anything* — can substitute for God's sovereign place in our lives.

Nothing replaces His love, His relationship, His finishing in us. That is why so many people — Abraham, Jacob, Moses, David, Elijah and Elisha, John the Baptist, Jesus and Paul — followed God for a time into deserts (think wildness) to know God. They fell in love with Him. And somewhere in the desiccated landscape of craggy valleys and dryness, they came to see God's largeness, and their smallness.

Today, we drive across deserts in comfort. We glint at the sun through sunglasses with the top down on a convertible. We drink bottled water, and we consult a GPS to see how many more minutes before we pass through the heat — if everything works. We think little of deserts.

But when we wake up in a desert! Our lips, encrusted with salt, are cracked so that the salt we taste is our own blood from our bleeding lips. The sun sits atop a brassy sky, and as far as we can see — all shimmers in the heat — featureless, hopeless.

God's Desert(s) and Finishing School

How could this happen? How could it happen to ME!?

Today deserts seem more inconvenient: places where we don't want the air conditioning to break down. Our deserts are *on the way* to the mountains or skiing or resorts or wine country we want to visit. But for our predecessors, those barren places posed one last, supreme test on wagon trains headed west to California. They were a dangerous, lethal block *in the way* of settlers headed to Oregon. They had to cross and survive this terrible test to reach their promised land, their dream of a new life.

Let's make two distinctions.

Distinction 1: We can cross our fingers, try and dodge the issue by saying — God *permits* deserts. Really? If God permits them, then who *authors* them? Who can create but the Creator? Driven by needs we never asked for, and couldn't create, we use the nature or personality God gave us — neither good nor bad but capable of both — to steer us, to steer our choices. He promises us He is working, using all of it to perfect us as His children, 24/7/365.

To develop more and more of the good from our needs, He uses desert times, wilderness experiences to separate us from our grave clothes, religious rot, and worldly viruses.

Distinction 2: Some of us think *we create* deserts in our lives. We author them with alcohol, abusing ourselves or those close to us, running to our own gods, or from God. People use their imagination. Not a lot, but enough to feel like they are in control. Not so. God authors all creation, all reality, and every desert. So, every desert holds a promise. Breathe that in. A promise.

As God authors all deserts (wild, we know), then they hold a promise a possibility. Consider Solomon sliding into his desert. He fell from having God talk to him and grant him everything until he said it all tasted like sand: "all of it is meaningless!"[99] But then wisdom for "Solly" rose back up: "to everything there is a time."[100] He saw a purpose in a desert!

I want you to see Me

Take Moses. He murdered an Egyptian overlord and saw his only place to run was into the desert. He messed up his life. Maybe he thought he created a desert and ran to it — right into God's waiting arms. Moses moved in with one of God's priests, married his daughter, took up tending the priest's sheep, and unwittingly preparing to tend God's nation.

For forty years in a desert God separated Moses from Pharaoh; making him nobody to become God's somebody; and another forty leading a people to become a nation — in a desert! God had astonishing purpose in His desert for Moses.

Here is a wonder: we camouflage a desert's purpose by thinking we created it! We must be Lord of a desert we made!

Not so. We are lord of nothing. God is Lord of all. Many of us know we didn't make a desert, but miss that God no less calls us into them.

Hear it another way: no one accidentally wanders into a desert. God creates it for a purpose. He causes it to look however I want it to appear — I choose a camouflage for His hand — until He perfects me in it. He even works in the camouflage to get me to a place where I see my life is all about Him.

God designs. God calls. God leads men and women into wilderness. We are in for a time, to accomplish His purposes. When we finally see a desert as a beautiful instrument to clean us, separate us from lies, and deepen our love for God; we see God's Glory in the place. For many, if we get this; we come to a peace, regardless of pain, and understand we're not in a separating place for our past. We're here for our future, for His Glory. Things may even get easier.

---

[99] Ecclesiastes: 12:8 "Meaningless! Meaningless!" says the Teacher. "Everything is meaningless!"

[100] Ecclesiastes 3:1-8.

God's Desert(s) and Finishing School

Jesus, as forerunner for us all, was led by the Holy Spirit to His desert encounter with God — and with Satan: God's work, Round 2! Father finished the Son's complete dependence on God, the Word, and the Spirit before dispatching Him on His mission. Jesus was equipped with everything we have.

Look at two more people in their deserts.

Elijah finished his highest accomplishment, ending Baal worship in his country — and ran to a crashing depression in a wilderness. God met him, fed him, and led him *further* into desert — to its very heart: to the mountain of Moses! In a few astonishing minutes, Elijah saw earths' greatest powers are not fire, nor wind obliterating rocks, nor earthquakes leveling mountains. No, earth's greatest power lies in God's Spirit speaking to us — quietly — when we finally hear His voice in stillness. God cleans waxy buildup and noises until we hear Him powerfully speak.[101] It is God circumcising our hearts.[102] His power reshapes the world. When God finished Elijah in the desert, just like us, God dispatched him back to change the course of two countries.

One last example: John the Baptist loved the desert so much that he never switched back to civilian clothes or civilian diet.[103] He even commuted to his day job as a preacher and baptizer, to return home to the desert each evening.

In old time preaching, preachers described deserts as wilderness experiences.

We don't often find wildernesses across the street from lush gardens. Palm Springs does not count. Turn off its water and it will dry into desert in a year! No, we descend into deserts slowly. Snow and vegetation, then low scrub trees, bushes and sparse vegetation;

---

[101] Much like circumcising baby boys, God calls this circumcising our hearts.

[102] Deuteronomy 10:16 "Circumcise your hearts, therefore"

[103] Matthew 3:4.

I want you to see Me

In God's geography, deserts aren't "on the way" or "in the way."

Deserts
Wildness
Wilderness
Solitude

are His ways to achieve great things in people He loves and uses.

and then further in, beetles dig into sand to survive, microbes may be the only living thing for miles, and the same dune fries you at noon and freezes you at midnight.

On entering a desert:

Gary: It was 1984 and my wilderness experience began slowly, gradually.

Back in '79 I ran for Congress. Afterwards I made it clear to my family and close friends that I would not do this again. But I did. Listen closely to how this came to be.

Before I filed to run in '81 the second time, I was in DC with my pastor for a Christian march on the White House and we visited the House of Representatives' gallery, watching Congress in session. It deeply affected my pastor. I didn't know why. We didn't discuss it.

I had not thought of running for Congress again. In fact, I had repeatedly stated that I was opposed to running again. We stood in the Gallery. I said nothing. He said nothing. We returned home. He quietly asked three deacons to join him weekly to pray that I would hear God's voice concerning this. He didn't mention the weekly meetings to me.

One morning I had my quiet time,[104] and then read in the paper where Congressman Synar had voted his "liberal way" on an issue. I sensed God nudge me to run.

---

[104] It is a time when Gary reads passages from the Bible, prays, and reflects on God and what He is doing in Gary's life.

God's Desert(s) and Finishing School

I called my pastor for lunch and over lunch revealed my shocker: I sensed God nudge me that morning to make another race for Congress — and I didn't want to do this. My pastor's eyes brimmed. Tears dripped down his cheeks.

God is using it all: period.

I asked, "Why? What is this about?"

Only then did he relate *seeing* me working on the floor of Congress while in the gallery, and how deeply it affected him. He further told me that on our return from DC he and three deacons began meeting weekly in prayer over this.

It was my turn to be shocked.

I invited five families to join him and his wife at our home on the following Saturday night as the filing deadline was days away. They agreed to pray with me about this for two days and return on Monday night to share what they believed they heard from God.

Sunday was strange. In the Bible lesson, Jesus walked by the seashore to tell Peter, who was having no success fishing, to cast his net otherwise. Peter caught a ton of fish. Jesus chose Peter to follow Him, but only after God made Peter successful. I sensed God show me that in spite of the success in my law practice and not wanting to interrupt it again by running for political office, that this was about God — not me.

My mistake was thinking my success was about me, not God. Ouch. He clearly showed me differently that Sunday morning.

That Monday night, to the person, each person gave a positive thumbs up! Everyone concluded that I would be the next congressman. They believed God had shown this to them, and some had a scripture to back it up.

They enthusiastically said it whole heartedly, believing it. I ran. I was defeated. And that was unsettling, but it did not seemingly throw me for a loop.

109

I want you to see Me

Outwardly I still functioned, but inwardly it hit me deeper than I knew 'til later. It hurt — not that I wouldn't go to Congress — but that I *missed* God. Back then I believed we might miss God. I believed my friends had heard from God, so the only other possibility was I was unworthy of His calling for me. I still saw me as sovereign, so I bore the brunt of unworthily missing God's call.

Another public defeat did not derail me or my life trajectory — that I could tell — that I could tell *at the time.*

But in the same way a tiny burn of a few seconds on a space probe like Juno hurtling through space to Jupiter will make a difference of millions of miles a few months later, the sense that I might miss God was nudging me to a desert; still years away. God had begun working deeply, deeply in me.[105]

He began to separate what people (however godly or important) say to me from what God says to me. In deserts, God separates things. This was huge for me. I thought I knew how to listen for God's plan for me, but I had to realize God's plan **is happening**. Period. God is using it all. Period.

I had listened, I wanted to hear people say, "His plan *may* be this" but I was still short of — seek counsel, but listen only for God's still small voice. His voice only. I needed a desert to separate everyone else's voices from His!

So my defeat did not waylay me, because I was raised by a man of God — the real thing. He was "Bill" to everyone because they wanted to feel close to their pastor. Imperfect? Certainly, but amazing in my eyes as both father and hero. Maybe you weren't raised by a perfect father. Neither was I, but as clearly as I saw dad's imperfections, he was still perfect in my love for him. I know. He did the best he could, with the needs he had.

---

[105] I was coming to understand Isaiah 26:21. That many things we might be tempted to take credit for, God was doing to His glory. We get confused when we conflate our accomplishments with His glory.

God's Desert(s) and Finishing School

Subtly, God separated me from what I felt and was taught even by my father whom I admire so greatly. God was pushing me beyond how circumstances appear, to trust what God says using His Word or His still small voice in my spirit. I still struggle with that at times. Again, my desert began slowly.

Stop. Let's examine two ideas. First, what *causes* deserts, wildness, or these wilderness experiences?

See where I say "my desert began?" If you go to counseling, good counselors can tell you much about your desert. Therapy can chart your desert's geography and weather — translated your past, your family, and your baggage. But counseling typically can't help you answer the *why* question.

Some people endure what you endured without a desert! Others have it much worse, bereft of hope they end their lives, or are institutionalized. Only He Who makes deserts and calls us through them can tell us *why*. Only He can tell us *why* severity comes to some and not others, and why some deal with deserts so differently.

If you are a parent, you know. More unique than each of our fingerprints, we as God's children resemble our own biological children. Do we raise each child differently? Yes. So does God. Why? He gave us different personalities and natures, and different ways of reacting to problems, stress, or challenges. Finally, God holds different purposes for each life. Each purpose requires different preparation and perfecting in view of how He will use each of us.

Second, see above where I said "my search for Truth?" In a previous book, *The Apple*,[106] I spoke at length of my search for Truth. In *Apple* I continually stumbled, got up, walked, ran, fell, crawled, got up and fell backwards — but always — hungering for Truth. My progress has always been *towards* Truth: God's Truth.

God loves Truth so much He named it for His Son. That's right, Truth has a face and a Name — and it is Jesus. So how much Truth

---

[106] *Thank God They Ate the Apple!* Gary Richardson, 2008.

I want you to see Me

do we find in deserts, or anywhere for that matter? In a desert God does not grade on the curve, He heals and calls us based on the Truth we absorb, and He already knows what we will take in out there. He has already designed every parcel of Truth He intends us to learn in the time in the desert.

Does God only use deserts? No. He uses mountain tops so high, and He uses valleys, no matter how low. These all occur; these all bear His design. These all perfect us for the Kingdom because; it is beyond what we do and don't do in deserts that bring God glory. In deserts, beyond what we do. We're the product. We are the point. As we know Truth more, God polishes and buffs us to reflect Truth, to reflect Jesus in us — to bring God glory. Okay, now I am ahead of myself.

Back in '79 I accepted an appointment as a Federal United States Attorney. U.S. Senator Don Nickles offered it three times. The first two times I turned it down as I didn't want to further interrupt my law practice. The third time I accepted and filled the office in May, '80. That appointment by President Ronald Reagan lasted four years until May, '84.

Fast forward to '84's August where in Oklahoma, as usual, it was hot and dry, and much like the weather, I found myself unsettled and had no idea why.

Something in me was drying up. My life felt unfamiliar — I didn't know. Hear it again. I didn't know. Hear it this way, I had no idea what was happening in me or to me. I had become that ship on the ocean with no rudder. I arose every morning with a lump in my throat as if I had just swallowed a huge question mark! It stuck in my throat. That question mark hung over my thinking, lurked over everything.

Something in me was drying up.

I asked my pastor to lunch. Hot outside, we lingered over lunch as I struggled to put

God's Desert(s) and Finishing School

into words — this thing encroaching on my life; this dryness clamping down on my heart. On my lunch and in my being, I was choking! Only one gulp of sand in a desert chokes you.

Even sitting here thirty years later, writing, I find myself quietly weeping to look back and see God's hand in all things — yes, even this. How hard it was for me and may be for you to see that God authors what doesn't look, feel or taste good. God authors, God allows, God construes — any way you need to say it — for His purpose(s).

I struggled to put it into words for my pastor. I repeated that I was losing my love for the things of the church. Today I would say losing my passion. But I didn't know enough about what was happening to recognize this was about my passion.

God had begun separating me from *church* as a savior. Truth has a Bride called the church, but His Bride; His church can never substitute for knowing the Groom: Jesus. He alone is full Truth. I know that now, many years later, but back then I didn't. Not knowing was like standing over an abyss, trying to describe falling in. I could not fashion words for it. Like a thirst for something I had never tasted, I could not describe what dissatisfied me, much less if an answer existed. I didn't know enough to know that maybe God had placed a craving that was defying description in me.

I did not understand it. I could not put it into words and that brought something new — nameless fear — anxiety. I was scared. I told my pastor that I felt like I "was headed 'south,' on a slippery slope . . . out of control."

It scared me. I had watched men who loved the church slide *south*, sideways, or down. They didn't slip a little, they slid far. I so wanted a name for where I was headed: a place, a known reality. With no idea where I was sliding, I was terrified. "South" is Texan for slipping far into dry, possibly lawless, even crazy places. I felt I was losing control on a slippery slope. A sand avalanche was swallowing me.

I want you to see Me

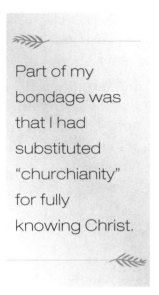

Part of my bondage was that I had substituted "churchianity" for fully knowing Christ.

I often said I was "losing my desire for the things of the church," and it is so strange now to grasp the root meaning of desert — a place of separation. Much later, I grasped that part of my bondage was that I had substituted "churchianity" for *fully* knowing Christ. Possibly, you know Christ and have never been through anything like this, yet! Thank Him for being gracious to you. He often allows us less devastating wilderness experiences. But God alone knows what we need to experience; what it will take to reshape us.

God was prying my fingers off my hold of *church things* substituting for knowing Him in His fullness. Don't get me wrong. Today I love Christ's Bride, and attend church regularly — moreover I worship, I wrestle with the Word and love my pastor. But even the church as an idol, as mere religion, must be separated from Christ, so that we can love Him first, alone, best.

During two lunches with my pastor, I only knew I did not know what to do. I wept over a slippery unknowing.

Now I know, as you may know but may forget; a *church* never saved anyone; just as a *hospital* never heals us. Hospital is where doctors, researchers, and nurses point us to medical truths, and apply them to us. Even lunching with my pastor, my local hospital's chief of staff; may have had some power, but no. I felt nothing.

I resigned from all I was doing at church: deacon, training union teacher, and two committees. My reason? "I am headed south, and don't want to bring embarrassment to the church." I languished. September turned out to be as hot as August.

Three weeks after resigning, I sat in the parking lot of my newly refurbished law office: still no rain. Workmen put on the remodel's finishing touches, as others unloaded new furniture. I sat in a new

God's Desert(s) and Finishing School

diesel Mercedes, oblivious to its new leather smell. I would never have bought it, knowing I was about to pull the plug on my finances.

The remodel testified to the firm's strong future to people. My life felt as thin as a coat of paint. I sat driving nowhere, and watching men carry my furniture into my law firm. God whispered, "You can't stay here."

It did not take long.

I walked in on that paper they leave on the carpet and talked to my partner, my brother-in-law, Lloyd. I heard me say, even as I had no way to explain it to Lloyd, me, or anyone else: "I can't be your partner anymore."

Lloyd's expression begged the question. I could only say, "I have no way to explain this to you."

Genuinely concerned, he asked, "What will you do?"

I lamely said, "No idea." It sounded ludicrous. I still said it, and had no idea what came next.

He could not help but ask, "What do we tell the people?"

I paused. "Tell them I am going to Tulsa."

Lloyd, "Are you going to Tulsa?"

Me, "I am."

Lloyd smiled to ask, "When did you decide that?"

The irony of it hit me as I said, "Right here. Now."

Lloyd then asked, "What do you have in mind concerning the law firm?" He asked since I owned 50 percent of our successful, small town law practice.

I said, "Lloyd, it's all yours. All I want is my share of the fee on the case I settled last week." I brought the case to the firm. I felt that this money from a death case would help me get a new start — a start *where*, my spirit was begging to know.

I want you to see Me

I left Lloyd's office, leaving all in his hands. I later received a fee from the case — smaller than I expected due to Lloyd's unexpected deductions from what I thought to be my share — but here, too, God made me start with less to depend on Him more, to learn it is all about His purpose in my life.

I had begun leaving parts of my life, and my leaving was moving into high gear. Life, this office, this day all felt surreal.

I entered my office to see a brand new desk I would never use. It was as pretty there as it was in the store. It meant nothing. I felt I was in another man's office, and it soon would be.

The intercom on the new desk crackled to life startling me: "Bull Bradley is here to see you, Mr. Richardson." It was more startling as he came in to talk. Bull had no appointment, so it was strange, surreal to see his huge form crowd my door.

I had represented Bull in Waco, Texas, winning a hefty settlement against a bank. In the ensuing years, Bull became a second father to me. It was bizarre to see him walk in! I had no idea he was anywhere near Muskogee.

Bull said, "I'm traveling through town on my way to appointments up north."

I waited a sentence or two before I interrupted, "Bull, I am going to tell you something that will shock you. I am leaving the firm."

Bull caught his breath and responded; his voice gravelly with deep emotion, "Gary, you could not have told me anything to make me happier!"

I stammered, "What?"

He continued, "Two movers had trouble maneuvering your new desk through the door. They needed a third hand. While helping carry in the desk, I had an overwhelming sense: 'This isn't Gary's desk. It's his coffin!' "

God's Desert(s) and Finishing School

I can't say what I felt. I raced through a hundred emotions a couple of times apiece sitting there staring across the desk at a man who had been like a dad to me in this crazy world. God used Bull to tell me, long before I would recognize it, "I'm here with you, Gary. I authored this moment, and I am leading you through this desert."

How like me? How like you? How like us all? God shows us our life course is headed in a new direction, and even sends an announcer like Bull was for me, yet it is years before we see God authoring, leading — sovereignly directing our steps.

Bull had to go. I followed soon after never to return as part of the firm.

I had no idea how I would tell my wife, Shirley. Consciously, I had not planned a shred of this morning before it started unfolding. Unconsciously, I had been drifting to this place for some time.

What had begun as rumblings in '79 had become thoughts, then had grown into leanings over the last ninety days. Most of which I failed to detect.

I lay no blame or responsibility at Shirley's or Lloyd's or anyone else's feet. I'm not invoking *desert* or *God's sovereignty* to escape my responsibility in all that happened.

Days later, late in the evening, still confused and lost as to what was happening to me, I drove around Tulsa. Being in the city where I told Lloyd I was headed didn't help my soul's turmoil. I had no place to go and no idea how to provide for my family. What was I thinking? I carried a burden for my wife, my twelve-year-old daughter and two sons in college; and yet overwhelming me, consuming my heart was this *desert-for-which-I-had-no-name* engulfing me.

The word "desert" didn't even form in my mind. I knew where I was headed has no place on a map. I sensed business, family, and success being hammered into new priorities, new orders by God in me. They obviously weren't where God wanted them.

I want you to see Me

It was night. I drove west on 71st street between Harvard and Lewis. 71st was narrower, and I passed tree studded neighborhoods whose warm lights in the houses left me hollow. I drove up this long hill, pulling the weight of my failing life behind me.

I felt the hardest part fall behind me. Suddenly, the enormity of physically separating from all that was important to me — family, career, church, friends, security, reputation —all of it hit me. The enormity of so many losses hit as endlessly pounding waves. Then, almost as suddenly, I felt His presence. I was strangely safe. Secure.

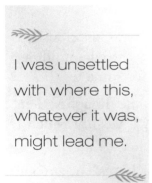

I was unsettled with where this, whatever it was, might lead me.

In a blur of emotions, my focus shifted to where I was headed. It seemed to be God and me. I know, God is not a *direction*. Reading this again after so many years, I still weep as I remember.

I was unsettled with where this, whatever it was, might lead. But in the night as I neared the top of this long hill, the weight somehow lessened.

I drove. I grieved, knowing I was causing others to grieve.

I felt the separation, and croaked out loud, "God, I have no idea where You are taking me, but if You are taking me to Reno Street in OKC, (Skid Row back then) I am ready to go."

I had always feared failure, and in my desert God was separating me from that fear. It didn't feel wonderful or beautiful. I trembled. I was lonely — and yet I sensed an inexplicable peace! As poorly as I had described anything to anyone, so I could not put what was happening in the car into words. I topped the hill to see lights twinkling in the distance in my night.

Maybe you think I found a way to relieve myself of my own responsibility.

God's Desert(s) and Finishing School

Maybe you think I theologically shifted my blame to God's plan for my life. Think again. I had carried my load of blame and massive responsibility for life, successes and direction until I washed up spent and battered on God's shore of sovereign abandon. Having lived with blame, I was astonished by — His peace behind the wheel that night. In this most difficult, draining, strange place my only sanity and hope was — even here, God was directing my steps.[107]

I did not stride ashore bravely like David hunting five stones, or Esther fasting to risk her life, or Moses peering into the Red Sea's dark waves. I did not come faith-filled like Noah or Joshua. No, I trudged ashore spent with a stench of slavery like John Newton when he cried out to God on his own slave ship.[108]

I hadn't come to Tulsa *for* anything. I simply came, and I didn't know *why*, much less *that* God was completing something in me. I knew of no reason to leave my wife, three precious children, church, friends and law firm; and my reputation? I could hear people, "Why yes, our fine, upstanding US Attorney appointed by Ronald Reagan just up and left his family and practice and is driving around Tulsa. No job. No prospects." Crazy in people's eyes and mine as well.

Hear this, please. However unsettling it felt to me and may feel to you. It is neither unsettling nor unknown to God. Nearing the top of that long hill that night in that car on 71st Street, I began to sense a peace only God gives, and the vanquishing of fear that His peace brings.

I hadn't the faintest idea what was happening, but God did, and however imperfect, deficient, and defective my understanding or life — I trusted that. I was glad no one was in the car to grade me, assay my faith, or correct me. I was alone in a car with God. Maybe that's why He takes us to deserts, because no one can interfere, or

---

[107] Psalm 37:23.

[108] In a violent storm in 1748 aboard his slaving ship. Newton later penned "Amazing Grace."

I want you to see Me

try to represent Him, or steal away a shred of our depending on Him in the moment.

Suddenly I sensed no fear. I breathed. After all, in my life what could be worse than this? For the first time in my life, I did not fear failure, even if it meant Skid Row. I knew that in the eyes of people I was experiencing profound failure driving in that Mercedes so lonely.

I drove.

In all of Tulsa, I knew two people: one a client and the other an old friend from the insurance business back in the seventies.

My client Chris had a one bedroom apartment that he only used when he was in Tulsa from Dallas. On learning of my situation as we discussed his current case, he offered his apartment as a temporary solution. Low on cash, I accepted his gracious offer. Isn't this just like God? He is always (at least!) a step ahead of us in filling our needs. Not always as we might like them filled, but that's not His promise. He promises to never leave or forsake us. He promises to direct our steps, and provide our needs. And He always does!

At this point I was so lost, so clueless about what was happening in me that I hadn't thought much of where I would sleep! It was way down my list in my confusion.

It took little time to move into Chris's second floor apartment. No boxes and few clothes. I left on the spur of the moment, with no idea I was leaving, much less a plan. I was travelling light.

I remember that time as so convoluted; even how I opened a new law practice is a bit of a fog. I had little money and had just resigned as a US Attorney: after draining our savings to supplement my government salary. I was obligated for a sizable mortgage on a home in Muskogee, a new Mercedes and my two sons in college; one at Baylor and one at OU. I made these moves assuming I would soon settle back into my financially successful law practice with Lloyd.

God's Desert(s) and Finishing School

Could it look bleaker? I returned to my practice for two months after serving as US Attorney for four years. I walked out; left the practice and my fifty percent ownership. I left my wife, daughter, church, friends, and what reputation I had; and moved to a city where I knew two people. Driving a new car with no job and no way to make a payment pretty much killed the joy of that new car smell.

Bleak. It looked so bleak. Did I have total faith God would pull me through all this? I can't say an absolute "yes." He was building that faith in me. It all had its purpose.

I can't say "yes," but I had an inkling. I began to see that God wanted me where I had no one else, no place nor thing to which I could turn. God wanted me — here.

I can say I knew He would not leave me alone or abandon me, as did many friends. If I was reading their books, I sense many saying, "Gary abandoned us!" I understand.

Either way, I was alone. I felt helpless.

Yet He did pull me through all this, and poured out a blessing in the next eight years' successes as a trial lawyer to make more money than I had thought possible in a lifetime; starting with a national record-setting verdict of $58 million for my friend and former District Attorney, Vic Feazell, in a defamation case in Waco, TX.[109]

But backing up. I started a law practice in Tulsa. I opened a small office with no secretary in three small rooms. Soon my friend, Linwood Smith, called from Dallas. Linwood asked me to serve as in-house counsel for his newly-formed insurance operation. He asked if I had time. Time was all I had. He placed me on a $5,000 per month retainer and all I had to do was go to Dallas each Monday, at his expense. I could do that.

---

[109] It stood as the record settlement in a defamation case in *The Guinness Book of Records* for years.

I want you to see Me

Next, a few small cases trickled in from radio advertising. I hired a secretary and young lawyer fresh out of Law School to handle those.

A couple of months later, one of Linwood's friends, Jim, needed my Oklahoma contacts to expand his employee leasing business into Oklahoma. He simply had to show a presence in the State so he put me on a $5,000 monthly retainer as his in-house counsel, paid for my office, paid for my secretary that we now shared and provided our insurance.

Within ninety days, God had provided a new life. It was all God. I could never have known or planned all this. Again, as He was showing, any success was about God, not my talent. Many talented and intelligent lawyers are not blessed so much.

Even so I felt I had lost control of my life. Even making money — I felt lost and directionless. God used two $5,000 retainers per month that I neither hustled nor won to show me His sovereignty. He provided. He did what I could never have made happen.

In a desert no place felt like *home* to me.

Also, in a desert no place felt like *home*. I found no place of total rest or refuge. I cried out on lonely nights, "God, please let me feel Your presence!" Previously, when I felt His presence, I was *home* no matter where I found myself.

God provided beautifully, as only He can in a desert; all eleven years. But His provision in ninety days of coming to Tulsa: retainers, office, secretary and insurance overwhelmed me. I gave one day a week in Dallas and provided a businessman an Oklahoma business address; and was free to practice law. Don't try to make sense of it. I still can't grasp God's miraculous ways. He feeds nations and falling lawyers in their wilderness experiences.

But I still reeled from losing all the good things God had provided and now was *separating* from me. Had I made good things my idols?

God's Desert(s) and Finishing School

I was making plans as He instructs in Proverbs,[110] and leaving results to Him; but an unbearable pain held me: a pain of loss. Yet, mingled in that pain a deep, settled peace — inexplicably emerged as stars shine on clear nights for anyone leaving the glare of city lights and seeing stars for the first time!

If you have passed thru a wilderness, been stuck in a desert, you know what I know. God, just as promised in His Word, was directing my steps while separating me from idols — so many things I had put before Him.

Maybe you believe that anything God does in our lives will always appear good in our eyes. Not true, but He always uses it for good, even when it looks bad to us. That biblical lesson awaits your study if you don't trust our words.

God was sovereign in my life long before I knew it. As an infant has no ability to speak, yet lives in her parent's love and provision, so we live in God's control and loving provision before we possess words to express His care! How true for all of us is that? Jewish scriptures shout and whisper: "God is sovereign! He's in control!" Somehow as grace came in the New Testament, we lost track of how sovereign God still is.

What can I say? Deserts are terribly featureless. Bedouins and others, who navigate them with no GPS, amaze me. I wondered successful and empty for eleven long years. In a desert you can walk for days, and the mountains dancing on the heat in the distance appear not one inch closer than last year.

I walked as if in a dream — sometimes nightmare — for eleven years: from late '84 to '95. It is painful to say, but I entered a bad marriage with what I considered to be a beautiful lady who I could show off on my arm: wrong motive. We met in Sunday school at a Methodist Church in Tulsa. I desired beauty; little else mattered in my desert. But I never saw myself as a victim to my second wife, my

---

[110] Proverbs 16:9.

I want you to see Me

former law partner, or anyone. I clearly see God is who He says He is: so I am only a *victim*, in a good sense; to Him. He clearly says He "directs the paths of the righteous" — His Children. If you are His child, He has made you what all your striving and religion could never make you: righteous. We are righteous because our Heavenly Father says so.[111]

Let me tell you a few things about desert/wilderness times, based on my experience, as I grow to grasp more Truth from God's Word. In a bewildering desert it does not matter how often I ask God, "Why?" If He hasn't finished using this wilderness to perfect me as He desires, answers won't come, yet. Maybe answers come after He brings me through it. Only after He finishes using a desert to finish all in me He set out to accomplish — Only if I am completed enough — Only if He is ready to let me leave a desert does He start to divulge His purposes, His thoughts, His intentions.

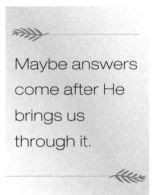

Maybe answers come after He brings us through it.

Immediately after releasing me from the desert and renewing me, God tenderly gave me answers to my "whys." I had begged, "God, in the long, lonely nights when I cried to feel Your presence, why couldn't I?"

He whispered, "You weren't ready, son. I had more work to do in you that I chose to complete in a wilderness experience — and I wasn't far enough along that you could understand."

That left me reeling. He continued, "I was there, but you had not arrived at the place I was taking you."

I learned in our orchard as a boy that fruit often appears ready for picking — before it is ripe. Fruit picked prematurely has little taste, little value, and can't finish ripening. So are our deserts. We *know* we're ready to come out from under the pain and adversity. But we're not ripened and God knows the time of our finishing.

---

[111] Romans 8:1-3; Romans 8:10.

God's Desert(s) and Finishing School

And, at harvest's end we look back to see God's wisdom and timing. Maybe in His sense of humor He repeats Himself to point out to us later — "I was ready to talk. I actually spoke to let you feel My presence; to hear Me, but you weren't ready to listen! I've been excavating your earwax for years! I spring you from a desert when you can finally hear! Can you hear Me, now?"

I now say, "Yes, Lord! And thank You for Your timing." Similarly I promise you, dear reader, that you won't hear His answers until you are finished enough.

He is ready for you to hear, but *you* won't hear it until you are finished enough, ripened, and able to hear.

Also in a desert, it matters not how richly you felt His presence before. No memory of feelings follows you in a desert. You can't live on feelings in a desert. Past emotions vaporize on the dancing heat waves shimmering in the distance. You can't live on the past. The past is desiccated, only a mouthful of dust remains.

And finally, I can say we *decorate* our deserts. We aren't finished enough to hear His voice. We're going nowhere. We don't sense His presence. We're in doubt — so we decorate! We buy nice houses, cars, vacations, and install pools in the deserts of our soul. We take pictures with important people. We put things on our office walls to say, "I am someone! *I am relevant!* See!?"

Do not resist or run from your difficulties.

These problems are not random mistakes; but hand-tailored blessings designed for our benefit and growth. Embrace all circumstances that I allow or bring to your life. Trust Me to bring good out of them. View problems as opportunities to rely more on Me.

If you start to feel stressed let those feelings alert you to your need for Me.

So, your needs become doorways to deep dependence on Me and increasing intimacy between us. Self-reliance is acclaimed in the world. Reliance on Me produces abundant living in My Kingdom.

Thank Me for difficulties. They provide protection from the idolatry of self-reliance.

—*Jesus Calling* by Sarah Young. May 10th devotional.

I want you to see Me

Even as we hang more mementos and successes on our walls showing our relevance, God whispers, "Don't you see Me — in all of this?"

Remember the people we studied in their deserts? A desert is to learn in and leave. Jesus left in forty days to save the world. He was perfected. Again, Moses left his desert in weeks of seeing and hearing God in a burning bush. He was doubtful, but obedient and ready for God to use.

Again, Elijah left his desert in minutes —not of feeling thunderous forces, but on hearing God's stillness talk to him. He was changed, renewed, more like God. John the Baptist never left a desert stillness. He loved it so much he left the crowds every evening and returned to it.

What of you? If God doesn't see you as finished, if you are not where He wants you, if not perfected enough, you simply won't look to leave a desert. Hate it? Maybe. Leave it? No. Not until God has you where He wants you.

If you are in a desert without recognizing sovereign God as Author of deserts, you may think, "I'm in charge of my time in the desert." To prove that lie, you hammer God *with* why. You try to recapture past feelings. You decorate a desert. Pretty silly.

So we decorate deserts, not knowing how long we will be stuck there. My desert decor was hollow, stifling, and sickly.

Today, my life is more beautiful than ever. I have a beautiful, loving wife, Lanna, who God sent to me. A wife, who is friend and companion, brings great joy. God and His work in our lives is beautiful beyond measure and it never ceases as He prepares us for the Kingdom.

I was on my way to seeing, on my way to experiencing emotionally as well as in my head two things. First, only in knowing God as

God's Desert(s) and Finishing School

sovereign, did I cease being anxious.[112] Second, only in struggling, and in the thick of struggling seeking to renew my mind as Paul related[113] did God establish His peace in me.

I might soon leave my desert, I hoped. I still had not learned something at this point God knew I needed. God calls us into these experiences and in His time (His alone), as He knows when we are like fruit ready to be picked (He alone knows), He will bring us — more complete — out of the desert. We never know the day. Or the time. Or the year. Just like starting a lab.

---

[112] Philippians 4:6 In nothing be anxious; but in everything by prayer and supplication with thanksgiving let your requests be made known unto God.

[113] Romans 12:2 Do not be conformed to this world, but be transformed by the renewing of your mind, that you may prove what is that good and acceptable and perfect will of God.

7

Finish and Leave the "Lab" of this Desert Experience

*"That's the excitement in obedience,
finding out later
what God had in mind."*
—Brother Andrew, *God's Smuggler.*

Gary: emerging from a desert experience was just as strange as going in. My exit simply, surprisingly occurred, but not before two more brutal losses. I lost an election for the governorship and after five years, the grating loss of my marriage was grinding to an end.

Backing up, as the summer of '95 grew warmer, something continually tugged at me until I informed my law partners I was headed to my house in Arrowhead, Colorado.

I didn't know when I would be back.

God was tugging on me, drawing me to the end of this desert, and yet I could not have told you that. I had no idea what was eating at me, drawing me away. My partners asked why I was leaving. All I could say was, "I have to go find myself. I have lost me." I know. On paper it looks like a sad line from a bad seventies movie, doesn't it?

I want you to see Me

Looking back, I had only lost the *part* of me God wanted gone for His reason. My problem was this *part* of me had become so much a sense of who I was that I thought it was essential to me being me!

More and more, as I walk with God I now see that it is all about His perfecting us for His Kingdom and in the meantime, using us for His glory and purpose.

As I prepared to leave for reasons I neither knew nor could articulate; one partner's wife visited a bookstore. She bought me a book authored by a California minister, who had just gone through a divorce. Once again, as with Bull Bradley sitting in my office in Muskogee; she said God spoke to her to buy me the book. He placed a reminder on this book's pages through her.

Once more, God had prepared another messenger.

On a note she wrote, "Gary, God told me to tell you He is not through with you, and that all you're going through — He is using for your good. The light you see at the end of the tunnel is not a train."

Now, God directed her to give me a book and a hope-filled note she placed in the book. This encouraged me. She spoke into my life; having no idea of my mammoth struggle. She was an angel, literally God's messenger. And I heard Him repeat his message through her: God is in control. He directs my steps — even steps I couldn't believe had happened — and didn't want happening.

The words on paper sent an echo haunting my thoughts: "Just trust Me." So our gracious God beckons to each of us children as we struggle. And we all struggle — continuously — some more than others.

She had never bought me a book. She dropped it at the front desk saying, "Please give this to Gary." She has never bought me a book since. Her one-time purchase held a weighty, specific purpose.

Finish and Leave the "Lab" of this Desert Experience

My flight to Colorado felt so lonely, and at the same time I drew on an inexplicable inner strength. If I was headed to find peace with God, He kept *that* surprise from me.

I deplaned, found my rental car, and drove Interstate 70 up out of Denver into the mountains, oblivious to most of the beauty. My busy thoughts crowded any view from my windows.

I arrived at our Colorado home overlooking mountains and a golf course, to find a Bible I seldom thought of — still in my book shelf. It took days to reach for it. Arrowhead's golf course is near Beaver Creek, and I usually relish playing it. Golf, too, was far from my thoughts. I was oblivious to our beautiful three-story house, the course, and surrounding vistas.

For those first few days only the book and its astonishing little note consumed my time. I read. I wept. I read and wept quietly. I read and wept aloud, crying out in racking sobs. I now see a deep cleansing God was finishing in my soul. He was completely removing a part of me He knew to excise.

> I read. I wept. I now see a deep cleansing God was doing in my soul.

In days I pulled down the Bible. I now dove in; luxuriating in it almost every waking hour. I consumed the book and the Bible. God used a book to chisel open my heart and start a breaking process. Now, with His Word He was easing me into His exit program from my desert.

I knew no markers for where I was in this breaking and cleansing. I knew no way to see it was almost finished. No tour guide said, "Only four more hours and you will be healed, sane, and alive again, Mr. Richardson — at least for this desert experience!"

"At least for this desert experience" means others follow. Thankfully, none were as severe as this in the house in the mountains, and none ran nearly as long. But see this — the reward(s) far outweighs any pain I endured in the desert / breaking / ending / cleansing.

I want you to see Me

I know this: once we see the rewards of a desert/wilderness experience, we come to welcome them. We embrace them like friends. Court them with caution and reverence. Recognize we hold no control over them: when they come or when they end.

I moved out; outside reading. I now drank in the beauty of this stunning green golf course before the dry peaks across the valley — and often felt His presence. Read that again — often felt His Presence — which I missed for eleven years. I had been bereft of that feeling, that sensation, that reality for eleven years.

And now, only now was it all worth it. After leaving and feeling foolish. After feeling so alone! After days of reading and weeping, I again experienced God's presence in ways I had not known for eleven years of desert, in defeats and divorce. He restored me. I experienced a profound praise for God.

First, I had to sit and absorb that.

Then I had to phone some people. I called my children, my mom, my twin sister, many friends and family to say, "I only have a moment to talk, I have a lot of phone calls to make, I just wanted to call and tell you that I have come home."

No one asked what I meant. They knew. They all endured my struggles for those eleven years. My heart ached (still today) because in those desert years dad died. I know he grieved for me, his son, to his grave. I always sensed I was his pride and joy; and he was undoubtedly my hero. He walked among us as a handsome, strong man among men, a passionate preacher, self-educated and wise as any man I ever knew. And I let him down in his last days. Even so, God washed through me again, coursing through my heart and thoughts.

So hundreds of miles from my family and partners, I came home. How can you tell a difference? How different does a *desert* feel from *being home*? I do not know if I can explain, but I will try. For years I felt as if I had lost control over my life. Increasingly, I

Finish and Leave the "Lab" of this Desert Experience

made millions of dollars, and bought more things, and yet all of it left me feeling as if I were spinning out of control.

Sensing that sapped my strength. My mood and loss of strength stole my resolve. I no longer believed there was anything I could do. I no longer owned wisdom to plot a way out of this desert that separated me from all hope. I was lost — again — always. I still attended church, while in the desert, as I didn't want to think I strayed too far from God. He blessed my law practice and I made millions, so I must be doing well, right?

God, kindly and mysteriously, confirmed I really had come home. He used small, powerful and meaningful things so perfectly. He used things I missed in the desert, or whose meaning eluded me in that time.

I made so many calls that day telling people who knew and prayed that I had come home.

The next day God whisked memories of Larry Patrick into that otherwise empty house in Arrowhead.

I met Larry while beginning my desert, after drifting from Muskogee to Tulsa. We were both single, had time on our hands, and I found him to be a very savvy Gin Rummy player: one of the best I played. I love the game — any game requiring strategy, so we filled evenings salving the pain as I trudged into my desert. Even after I married we continued our occasional game.

I recalled a warm but strange memory back in my desert, on an evening as Larry left our Tulsa home. I told my wife, "One day God will use me to lead Larry to Him." Instantly, the strangeness of saying it hit me. I wasn't sharing God with anyone those days. I couldn't believe I said it. It just came out. I wasn't even thinking thoughts like that back then, and was struck that I said it out loud! But I said it, and soon afterward Larry left Tulsa for Denver.

So I hadn't thought of or called Larry for five years. God gently whisked his memory across my mind again. It took a while, but I

I want you to see Me

found a Denver number for Larry, called him and he answered on the second ring. "Larry, I am alone for a few days at our place in Arrowhead. How about coming up for the weekend? We can watch some March Madness basketball; enjoy good food, and Gin Rummy. What do you say?"

He came. We watched hours of basketball, played a lot of cards and enjoyed great meals for three days. Suddenly Sunday morning arrived: time for Larry to leave.

We enjoyed breakfast. Larry was packed. Before he left we were savoring a last cup of coffee when he popped a question; as if it had been on his mind for some time. "Gary," he said. He seemed apprehensive, about to broach a new place in our friendship.

He asked, "I've noticed something really different about you — in you. May I ask what is going on?"

I felt a small shock. Even after all the startling moments of the past days, I hadn't considered it would be obvious to someone else! I had mentioned nothing to Larry for three days — nothing that was happening in me. Yet he saw. I had to drink that in.

I asked, "Do you have time for me to answer your question? I prefer not to try to answer it quickly, if you don't have time. I might take several minutes."

"I can stay awhile," he said.

I began. I shared my life before my wilderness experience, filling in the parts of my life before moving to Tulsa in '84.

I walked through my desert years. I shared how we met while I was in my desert. Last, I shared my return home, home to peace with my Heavenly Father. I finished. He stayed with me, completely focused for fifteen minutes. Now, he was calmly weeping.

Tears dripping down his checks, it was his turn to explain. "Gary," Larry said, "I've never heard anything like this. Ever. I didn't grow up in Church. I've only been in Church three, maybe four times — all

Finish and Leave the "Lab" of this Desert Experience

on dates." We both smiled at that. He continued. "Gary, I just never heard anything like this. It sounds like you have a personal relationship with God. All I ever heard about is a lot of rules."

It was my turn again, "Larry, you're right. I am speaking of a personal relationship: one where real changes come about in your life." I also shared my growing realization: "But it's all because of Him and His work to do in us. He gives us new desires in how to live our lives."

He was still with me, "Larry, it won't be a perfect life, but it will be beautiful."

He still listened. I continued, "Larry, would you like to know God as your personal Savior?"

Smiling through his tears he said, "Yes, I would!" We prayed the sinner's prayer as he professed Christ as Lord that Sunday morning at the "church" on Arrowhead's golf course!

Larry was shopping in a bookstore only weeks before, and for the first time ever he found the religious books section, bought a book on the life of Jesus, and began to read. God prepared Larry for our morning conversation!

Now again, we parted. I walked him out to his car in the cool air and sunshine.

Larry pulled out of the drive, and only then, as he backed into the street as he had that night in Tulsa so long, so far back in my desert, did I recall what I said to my wife in that driveway! "One day God will use me to bring Larry to Him."

Chills from the morning and the moment rolled over me.

Has God ever confirmed His power, His plan, His moving in your life? I now had three: Bull Bradley in my office in Muskogee, a book from my law partner's wife, and now Larry Patrick driving back to Denver as a new brother in Christ!

I want you to see Me

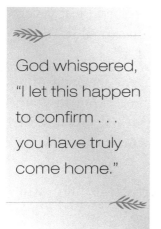

God whispered, "I let this happen to confirm . . . you have truly come home."

More than Bull's scary statement years before in my office, more than a friend giving me a book and note — to mark these days of healing and renewal, God whispered, "I let this happen to confirm . . . you have truly come home."

As his car disappeared I couldn't help but reflect on my smile when he asked me to share what was happening to me. God's confirmation washed through me, renewing me even more.

Standing in the driveway, I sensed that I was not *getting it* I was *getting **more** of it*. Two previous signs had come to me. This time God used me. Heaven's flood gates opened on me. From time to time God puts down markers in our lives, same as He did for Paul when Paul first set eyes on Ephesus. He assured Paul he would be back. My marker was driving home.

It was my turn to leave that hauntingly beautiful time at our Colorado home. I packed and got in the car to pull away and head to Tulsa.

I prayed for the whole two hour trip to the Denver airport. That was new. Flying back to Tulsa, God wrestled with me.

During eleven desert years, I kept asking my questions, like your questions in your desert. My favorite question was, "Why?" I so wanted to understand. Obeying Truth is everything, but I still yearned to learn more about me, my life as well as about Him.

I had four big questions for God. One: what happened to me back in '84?

Two: why did the divorce have to be?

Three: why on so many lonely nights as I cried out to You, did I not feel Your presence?

Finish and Leave the "Lab" of this Desert Experience

Fourth question: I have forgotten. Can I tell you how important that is? In dry times — answers seem *most* important — but as God restores us to Truth, to bonding with Him, some questions' importance fades away completely. I gladly traded no question for His presence!

God answered all *three* questions He intended that I remember. One, what happened to me in '84? Remember, I ran for Congress in '79 and lost. My pastor *saw* me on the House floor in session. Five couples saw me *win* in their prayers. Some backed it with scriptures. I lost. Losing revealed cracks in my foundation that widened until I broke apart in '84.

I sought God, and His silence convinced me again of a deep truth I knew as a believer. The Proverbs are succinct[114] — seek wise people's counsel. God showed me all these years later after a desert, "Counsel yes, but *direction* only from Me. Period."

Two: Divorce. God showed me things about me that broke me and then benefitted me, humbled me, and moreover pushed me to look to Him for my protection, and for the protection of those I love. They are from Him for me. It is enough that He answered me.

Three. "Why did You not answer me on those long, lonely nights?"

God said, "You still weren't ready. You still wanted the world's stuff more than you wanted Me." He made it obvious. I had focused more on my profession than on God's desires for me.

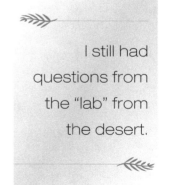

I still had questions from the "lab" from the desert.

So what do I know that I know about deserts?

God makes them.

God calls us into them.

---

[114] Proverbs 16:9.

I want you to see Me

God perfects us in them. He does not perfect us *only* if we want it. He is finishing us, period.

Thankfully, He is only finishing what He designed into that "lab," into that desert. If He did more, most of us would continually limp, moan or be overwhelmed!

If a desert experience seems harsh, then may you never learn how much worse spending your life would be attached to what is killing you spiritually.

> *A **note to you** — the things in you, your nature, your attitudes — some that you so dislike and for which you did not ask. You did not ask to be greedy, to be selfish, to have such a driving ambition for great success, to desire material things, or a strong need for control.*
>
> *None of us asked for these things.*
>
> *While in a wilderness, God works, healing the wounds in us that drive us to pursue these things. Know this. These too, the dysfunctional needs, have a place in our lives that God uses in ways we may never understand.*

SECTION 3

What difference does it make?

8

Living in Sovereignty While Here on Earth

*I wished God were like He used to be,
a few notches lower.
I wanted Him to be lofty enough to help me
but not so uncontrollable.
I longed for His warm presence,
times when He seemed more...safe."*
—Joni Eareckson Tada[115]

I leaned into the buffeting, chill wind. In the distance waves exploded on rock outcroppings, spending themselves to limp ashore quietly near me. Sunlight shone through waves as they raced at me flinging spray in the air. This sun setting over the Pacific was rising to warm Japan and the Philippines leaving me night's first shiver.

I was small. Time felt unstoppable and those distant shores seemed impassably far. And yet.

And yet, men lived and died sailing this ocean in outriggers, junks and ships, and then flew across this expanse in hops in hopes

---

[115] Eareckson Tada. J. (2012). *The God I Love: A Lifetime of Walking with Jesus*, Zondervan. Ms. Tada broke her neck in a diving accident and has been a quadriplegic since she was a teen.

I want you to see Me

of regularly scheduled transpacific flights. What seemed impossibly distant then, today has shrunk to a traveler's routine.

Technology's advance also shrinks distances: phones, surgical incisions, and the time it takes to do anything including write and publish this book.

Of all the shrinking trips, only one stands undiminished. Unshrinkable. It is still far. That trip stretches from where we live to death's other side, but here the Bible whispers hope. In its most passionate book, the Bible holds a marker, ". . . for love is strong as death…. Its flashes are flashes of fire, the very flame of the Lord."[116]

God charted the distance to death's other side. He built us a bridge for that time. More on that later, but what about now, today?

Francis Schaeffer's powerful book questions us: his question in the title still calls to us as we grasp God's sovereignty: *How Should We Then Live?*[117] We might add, how should we then live *earthbound?* Between today and heaven or hell for us all, we live on earth. We finish our days on earth. We then take the undiminished trip to death's other side.

As I grasp God's sovereignty, what *difference* does it make in living here on earth?

See it another way — created beings live on two planes: earth[118] and eternity. God rarely shows Himself **visibly** on earth since the Garden of Eden. Earthbound, I can't hop a plane to visit God, or see His daily heavenly news briefings, or catch His daily tweet. I **see** God as He acts: births, miracles, healings, and gorgeous sunsets —

---

[116] Song of Solomon 8:6, ESV.

[117] F. A. Schaeffer. (1976). *How Should We Then Live: The Rise and Decline of Western Thought and Culture.* Crossway, Wheaton, IL.

[118] This reflects our limited knowledge. It may be God created people on other planets and He is in fellowship with them in the way and to the degree that He has willed on those planets. C. S. Lewis and Madeline L'Engle both dealt with this idea in science fiction.

Living in Sovereignty While Here on Earth

but as the magnificent, ***visible*** Being,[119] only those in eternity ***see*** God. Stuck in time on earth, we don't easily see God. Do we pass from earthbound to eternity? Yes. We do. We all die. In our final trip we all pass to the next plane of living.

So we ask God, "How do we live and 'obey You, as You're obeyed in heaven?'"[120]

We know God is sovereign. Jesus and the Holy Spirit are completely enmeshed in Him. They fellowship in eternity. Angels see God on heaven's far shore; see His Glory in eternity. We feel that seeing God or His will is simpler for them.

Angels enjoy God in heaven or fear Him in hell, *seeing* His sovereignty. Beyond planet earth, they see firsthand. We see by faith.[121] God chose that we rarely ***see*** Him.

Many of us live life with no visual or up close and personal encounter — maybe good news! We might not survive encountering God. As He warned Moses,[122] we can't take it. God is too much.

First, we trust that as Christ followers, God commits to direct our steps.

So we live on the earth shore ***striving*** to the degree that we won't embrace God's sovereignty because we're locked in a marred version of human; born to die; sin in us; and using little of our brains to grasp a fleeting life! God shrinks any distance between Him and us as we wondrously see His sovereignty.

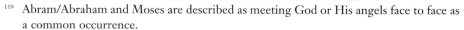

---

[119] Abram/Abraham and Moses are described as meeting God or His angels face to face as a common occurrence.

[120] Matthew 6:10 This is in Jesus' teaching on prayer, and speaks to us from His Model Prayer: "Come and set up Your kingdom, so that everyone on earth will obey You, as You are obeyed in heaven."

[121] Faith is the evidence of things not seen. Hebrews 11:1.

[122] Exodus 33:20 "No Man Can see My face and live," God said.

I want you to see Me

So how do we live on this shore and discern God directing our steps? First, we trust that as Christ followers, God committed to direct our steps —

God made a path for you.	All the paths of the Lord are mercy and truth.[123] He watches all my paths.[124]
You can know the path.	Teach me Your paths.[125] You will show me the path of life.[126]
God will reveal the path — to you.	The humble He teaches His way.[127] Who fears the Lord? God will teach him in the way He chooses.[128] I led you in right paths. As you walk, your steps won't be hindered.[129]

We are not the first people seeking to live wisely. Ancient people knew much. Some left amazing wisdom. Reading of those who lived courageously, even to the point of dying for believing God — we look humbly to what they thought about God was worth living for on this side of death — on this shore: earthbound.

We will start with *worthship.*

---

[123] Psalm 25:10.

[124] Job 33:11.

[125] Psalm 25:4.

[126] Psalm 16:11.

[127] Psalm 25:9.

[128] Psalm 25:12.

[129] Proverbs 4:11-12.

Living in Sovereignty While Here on Earth

Worthship. The Old English word for worship, *worthship*, asks "What is worth my time, worth my money, my allegiance — first place in my life? What is worth — worshipping?" It's the same question as, "How do we live here on earth, worshipping sovereign God?

To answer, let's survey two men's intertwined lives. They shepherded God's people past doomsday to see Him sovereignly protect His children. Firmly rooted in reality, they saw God's will powerfully. The two are bookends holding the wisdom of trusting sovereign God. They both worshipped God unreservedly.

Hezekiah: The first bookend

Answering the question of "How do I *worthship* sovereign God?" changed King Hezekiah. It changed his court and country. His story starts in worship.

As a teen he saw Assyria wipe away and scatter Israel[130] to the wind.[131] Later, on becoming king he worshipped God *religiously*, but Someone drove him many steps further.

God called Hezekiah to purify his worship. God moved Hezekiah to obliterate all gods worshipped by others. He scorched local sex-and-religion shrines,[132] and razed sacred groves where people held orgies.[133] He rid the Temple of a bronze snake like the one Moses lifted up in the wilderness,[134] because people began burning incense to it![135]

Through it all, "Hezekiah put his whole trust in God."[136]

---

[130] The ten northern Jewish tribes left the two southern tribes to form a nation earlier.

[131] 2 Kings 17:1ff.

[132] 2 Kings 18:4.

[133] 2 Kings 18:4.

[134] Numbers 21:9.

[135] 2 Kings 18:4.

[136] 2 Kings 18:5.

I want you to see Me

We won't glorify Hezekiah as a great man, but see God's assessment of his life: *"There was no one like him among all of Judah's kings — not before him and not after him. He clung to the Lord, never deviating from Him."*[137] Those kings included David and Solomon! God raised Hezekiah to a place He shared with no other kings. Obeying God, Hezekiah quit paying tribute to the Assyrian king who wiped Israel off the map! Hezekiah took back Philistine cities. God blessed every move.

God grew Hezekiah beyond worshipping His *blessings*. He preserved the scriptures.[138] He built ingenious aqueducts; purified the Temple; led a revival, and made priests clear the store rooms, so God would pour out a blessing.[139] God did.

And God held back any repercussions for ten years. Then He ushered Hezekiah into a lab marked *God's sovereignty*. Is it really marked: *Sovereignty of God Lab?* No. In the same way that your spouse is unlikely to say, "I'm hurting. Please remind me — why you fell in love with me?" but is far more likely to be shouting, sarcastic or depressed when she or he needs to hear that — *Sovereignty Lab* is not so clearly marked.

After getting rid of all idols. After seeking God and holding nothing in reserve. After eschewing politics, trusting God alone. After wholeheartedly following God — this. The Assyrian king stripped Judah's frontier fortress cities. Hezekiah caved. To pay off King Sennacherib, Hezekiah emptied his and God's treasuries. He melted gold from the Temple doors.

It only whetted Sennacherib's appetite. He sent his army under three commanders against Jerusalem. Hezekiah sent men versed in the Assyrian court's language to negotiate, but the three strutted below the wall loudly insulting the king, the people — and God —

---

[137] 2 Kings 18:5.

[138] Proverbs 25:1.

[139] 2 Chronicles 31:11.

Living in Sovereignty While Here on Earth

in the Jew's language![140] "How can you, Hezekiah, tell your people 'to trust in God' after you got rid of all the worship places?" Remember the sex and religion sites?[141] Then they ground it in: "God told my king to invade and take this place!"[142]

Sound contemporary enough? Today, some people ask why trust an ancient Bible. Others say, "God told me" to attack God's people!

God did not forsake Hezekiah. He grew another bookend, a prophet: Isaiah. God prepares as many as it takes.[143] Hezekiah heard the threats, ripped his robes, trudged into the Temple, and sent a message to God's man — Isaiah.[144]

Happened to you? You trust God is sovereign, but you feel so dirty, broken, or defeated that you ask *someone else* to talk to God for you? God let Hezekiah know how that feels. Hezekiah sent Isaiah a message, in case the prophet had missed the world's largest army spread below Jerusalem's walls!

> Has it happened to you? You trust God is sovereign, but feel so dirty, or defeated you ask *someone else* to talk to God for you?

How clearly did God show *this* prophet, Isaiah, His hand in history? Consider: Jesus quoted Isaiah more than anyone, and Jesus took Isaiah's title for Messiah: Son of Man. Isaiah saw God's sovereignty while reading Hezekiah's letter.

Hezekiah did better. Remember on the first threat, he stripped the treasuries to pay off Assyria's king? That is what people who know no sovereign God

---

[140] 2 Kings 18:21.

[141] 2 Kings 18:22.

[142] 2 Kings 18:25.

[143] Hezekiah actually heard Hosea and Micah as well.

[144] Isaiah showed Jesus would suffer and die for our sin in "the Suffering Servant Song" 52:13 – 53:12.

I want you to see Me

do. Now he forwards the Assyrian's message to God's man — Isaiah. He points out their blasphemies to Isaiah. Was he growing? Maybe we grow after emptying the treasury.

God's man, Isaiah, responds that these clowns will hear a rumor, go home and die. They do,[145] but God is not through working in Hezekiah. He now stands head and shoulders above every other king, but God is not through perfecting him! God is about to complete more in him!

Assyria's king himself returned with the world's largest army; surrounding Jerusalem like a million lightning bugs rising out of clouds of tents. His envoy brought Hezekiah a more pointed message. "Don't let this god of yours string you along! We have the gods of other countries in our carts. Did their gods help them against the King of Assyria?"[146]

Hezekiah awoke! Finally he knew what was *worthwhile*!

Worthshipping Sovereign God, he stood. He tore no robes. He sent to no one. Striding into Sovereign God's temple, he knelt before a tall, thick curtain behind which God visited. He spread the enemy's letter before God to say, "This one's addressed to You." It was finally all about God.

Hezekiah prayed, "God, seated in majesty on the cherubim throne. You are the one and only God, sovereign **over all** kingdoms on earth."[147]

If you hear nothing else from his prayer, hear "You're *sovereign over these our enemy*." And God is sovereign over yours as well. The rest of his prayer covers the obvious and asks God to save them.

God sent a message to an Assyrian king who would rape Jerusalem. "Zion's virgin daughter holds you in utter contempt.

---

[145] 2 Kings 19: 67.

[146] 2 Kings 19:11-13.

[147] 2 Kings 19:15, THE MESSAGE.

Living in Sovereignty While Here on Earth

Daughter Jerusalem thinks you're nothing but scum."[148] "[You] will not enter this city or shoot an arrow here, raise a shield, or build a siege ramp. By the way you came, you'll return. **I** will defend this city and save it."[149]

That's it. Hezekiah, complete before his sovereign God, *worthshipped* to discard all his and his country's idols; fearlessly bested old enemies and stood up to the earth's mightiest king. When confronted, he:

1. Did as the world does; paid off Assyria's King. He then

2. Did as religious people do; asked God's prophet to present his case to God. Finally, he

3. Knelt before Sovereign God to say, "This letter is addressed to You, Sir!"

Truest *worthship*. Truest *worship*. Sovereign God responded. Oh, did He! The next morning one in eight of Sennacherib's army awoke in eternity: 185,000 men. Terrified at so many dead men sharing their tents; the rest fled.[150]

Running for their lives, they left a few countries' wealth, breakfast on the spit, and tons of supplies — for "Zion's virgin daughter!" The enemy king ran home, never to go warring again, and be murdered by his sons!

Think. This line of reasoning may bother you. All Judeans suffered three attacks by the world's largest army as Hezekiah learned in God's lab. In our hyper-individualized world we hate it if each of us can't pay individually. We want each to pay on his or her *own* account *only*. Scripture shows how sin, learning, and healing carry high tabs — all partially picked up by others. Nations pay for

---

[148] 2 Kings 20:21.

[149] Isaiah 37:3-34.

[150] 2 Kings 19:35.

I want you to see Me

kings' excesses. A neighbor pays to hear another's screaming fights. A child for her father's abuses. The horror in a lab is sticker shock on learning sin's price tags.

Hezekiah in the Temple with that letter spread before God said, "I *worthship* You. I have no other gods, no other hope, Sovereign God!"

Do you have God's heart here? Hezekiah had His heart as he took a pompous king's letter to its intended recipient, and God rendered a stunning victory.

One last point. Assyria's king was right — partially. Isaiah: "Because [we Jews] have rejected [God's place], and rejoice in foreign fads, the Lord is about to bring against us . . . Assyria's king. . . . sweeping into Judah."[151] God did call Assyria's king to play a part, and then God dismissed him. God calls us all to play our part: maybe for salvation or perdition, but we will all be called! And we will respond!

Learn from Hezekiah. Wor*th*ship Sovereign God on our earthbound shore.

Isaiah: God's other bookend

Hezekiah was dying to self and living to God a process we know, hate, fear, trust, and cling to with all of our hope! Alongside him all the way was a prophet, Isaiah. In Isaiah 43, starting with verse one, Isaiah explains his following Sovereign God.

[1] The Lord says—

He who created you... He who formed you...:

"Do not fear, for I have redeemed you;

I have summoned you by name; you are Mine!

---

[151] Isaiah 8:69.

Living in Sovereignty While Here on Earth

[2] When you pass through . . . rivers, they will not sweep over you. When you walk through fire, the flames will not set you ablaze.

[3] For I am the Lord your God, the Holy One of Israel, your Savior ....

[4] "Here's how much you mean to Me! Here's how much I love you!"[152] I give people in exchange for you, nations in exchange for your life.

[5] Do not be afraid, for I am with you ....

[7] everyone called by My Name, whom I created for My glory, whom I formed and made."[153]

See what you may not expect, but will grow to love. Yes, Isaiah showed us God's sovereign protection in life's hardest episodes. It's easy to declare God's glory as blessings flow, but what if blessings dry up? God's promise stands even in our difficulties. He is God and Savior in blessings, but no less in dire times! That's too wondrous for words, but not for God! See God's point in sovereign protection: "Here's *how much* I love you!"[154]

Now look at Isaiah. Coming from a well-to-do family, he served as court preacher. He was young when his country lost confidence in the future.[155] He began having visions. He became God's prophet.

Isaiah warned of looming, sovereign judgment so Judah could escape, but it was too late. Regardless, he continued warning kings, but he also began a hopeful message for the people — in the future, after the inescapable judgment.

---

[152] Isaiah 43:4.

[153] Isaiah 43:5, 7 Smith, F. LG. Narrator. (1984). *The Narrated Bible: In Chronological Order*, Harvest House Publishers, Eugene Oregon. Tenney, M. C. Ed. (1975). *The Zondervan Pictorial Encyclopedia of the Bible.* Zondervan, Grand Rapids, MI.

Vine, W. E., M. F. Unger, & W. White. (1985). *Vine's Expository Dictionary of Biblical Words*, Thomas Nelson, Nashville, TN.

[154] Isaiah 43:4.

[155] Isaiah 43:1 "Isaiah" by J. Oscar Boyd in Volume III of *the International Standard Bible Encyclopedia*, J. Orr Ed. 1929 The Howard Severence Co., Nashville, TN.

I want you to see Me

Isaiah warned[156] of unavoidable, frightening times bearing down, but God promised to walk them through horrors and protect them to His glory. So Isaiah's words still hold hope for any one called by God. He points to God's sovereign glory — Who watches over us in frightening storms. No way of God showing His glory means more than Him saving us *in* a fire or flood. God's glory even allows us to flourish in those times. Isaiah:

VERSE 1 But now, the Lord says—	This prophecy is unlike any other.
He who **created** you... He who **formed** you...:	**bara** — He **chooses** *and* **creates** us.[156] God **fashions,** and **determines** us. Babies come with personalities, needs, and desires!
"Do not fear, for I have redeemed you;	God's work always banishes fear. Always.
I summon you by name. You are Mine!"	God chose Jews *individually.* No one hides in a mob.

God calls us by His name to say: "You're family," and "You can know Me!"[157] Paul will call this family — the elect.

Verse 2 "When you pass through waters, I will be with you;	God is present in overwhelming times.
when you pass through rivers, they will not sweep over you.	God saves us from being overwhelmed.
when you walk through fire, you will not be burned;	God is present in fires.
flames will not set you ablaze."	God does not let fires consume us.

---

[156] The people of Judah, the Southern Kingdom, the tribe from which David came.

[157] Isaiah 43:7 Heschel, A. J. (1962). *The Prophets*, Prince Press, Peabody, MA. Popper, W. (1931). *Volume II, Chapters 40-66, The Prophetic Poetry of Isaiah*, University of California Press, Berkeley, CA.

Living in Sovereignty While Here on Earth

Verse 3 Lord, God, Holy One of Israel, your Savior	All the titles — All sovereignty — so He can save us!
Verse 4 "That's how much you mean to me! It's how much I love you!"[158]	All of it to show God's loves for us.
I give people in exchange for you, nations in exchange for your life.	God **chooses** us — over others.
Verse 5 Do not be afraid, for I am with you.	God's love leaves no room for fear.

God's words through Isaiah thrill us. See them again, actually look at a few of the words. Let them come alive in you.

Isaiah 43:1 God's sovereignty marks the pinnacle of grace to the Jews. God lavishes His overabundant love on us to show His glory. God redeems *ga'al* us.[159] He bought us before we wandered off. He gave other lives in exchange for the Jews. Ultimately, the Lamb God gave in exchange for them and us is Jesus.

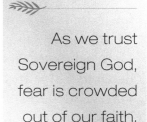

As we trust Sovereign God, fear is crowded out of our faith.

And now for the first verse's climax — fear not. *Yare'* means don't let anything cause us to fear including all the world's scary stuff. As we trust Sovereign God, fear finds no room in us. John said it perfectly after Jesus:

---

[158] Isaiah 43:4.

[159] Isaiah 43:1 BART and WordSearch 4, Copyright 1987-1996 NavPress Software, Austin, TX. This is the image of a kinsman redeemer as Boaz redeemed Ruth. Ellison, H. L. (1969). *The Prophets of Israel from Ahijah to Hosea*, Eerdmans, Grand Rapids MI.

I want you to see Me

There is no fear in love. But perfect love drives out fear, because fear has to do with punishment. The one who fears is not made perfect in love.[160]

Now **43:2** The Jews were desert not seafaring people. Crossing faraway rivers was scary. Worse, their lives on the other side of any river would be as Babylon's slaves. Fearfully, they trudged off to other gods' nations! They grew in faith to realize God was God over other gods, and then later that — there were no other gods! God said,

- He would be with them: His presence is our greatest comfort. (The absence of God's presence is called Hell.)

- No river could sweep over *shatap* them. They would not drown or be overwhelmed (their great fear).

- No fires would blister *kavah* them. This promise literally came true for Daniel's three friends.[161] They survived a furnace without getting singed for refusing to bow to a Babylonian king's image in front of thousands of people.

Now, add **43:3** God reminds us of His Name. God's Name is a promise — His guarantee of any promises. God's Name, *Savior*, calls for more than a "no-go-to-hell" thing. God repeatedly saves in *this* world. Isaiah saw this come true watching Assyria's king,[162] bypass Hezekiah even when he was angry with him. Senacherib stormed down to Egypt to shatter Pharaoh. God gave Egypt in exchange for Hezekiah. Hezekiah paid a fine. The Jews were untouched.

Now look at **43:4**'s amazing news.

- God said His people were precious *yaqar* to Him. *Yaqar* means heavy or glorious (in 43:7)! God's *heavy glory* gives

---

[160] 1 John 4:18.

[161] Daniel 3:8ff.

[162] "Sennacherib" by A. T. Clay in Volume IV of *the International Standard Bible Encyclopedia*, J. Orr Ed. The Howard Severence Co., Nashville, TN.

Living in Sovereignty While Here on Earth

heaviness. In the coming turbulent storms, *heavy* kept them from getting blown away!

Now add **43:5** God directs Isaiah to repeat "Fear Not."

- By God's grace, He shifted the basis of our relationship to Him from fear (based on what happens) to grace (based on Who He is.) The only "thing" in the universe we might fear — loved us first!

It gets even better: **43:7**

- God will bring back "everyone called by My name, whom I created for My glory." We, all of us, have someone we love *out in the storm* and this establishes our hope: God has ordained to bring them back to Himself.

God displays His glory in the stars, in the clouds, and in the beauty of our national parks — but ***nowhere like He shows it in His sovereign care and love for you!***

Our faith is in the sovereign God, Who sustains us in our challenges to solve them. Our only alternative to desperate faith is despair. Instead of giving up, faith holds on. It prevails. Do you know this hymn of desperate faith that underscores how we can live out believing in a sovereign God?[163]

"When obstacles and trials seem
Like prison walls to be,
I do the little I can do
And leave the rest to Thee.

"And when there seems no chance, no change,
From grief can set me free,

---

[163] Rev. S. Chadwick. From "the Will of God" F.W. Faber in a *Victorian Anthology 1837-1895*, Ed. E. C. Stern Cambridge, Riverside Press.

I want you to see Me

Hope finds its strength in helplessness,
And calmly waits for Thee."

Trusting God's path connects us to Him while we live "earthbound." *Worthship*, transforms us to see his sovereign work in our lives. So while living here, how else does God connect us to eternity, to better see how He works? Prayer helps.

Eliezer's practical prayer

One of the Bible's first recorded prayers comes not from a major player, but his servant. Abraham dispatched his servant, Eliezer, with a chunk of his wealth back to family in Ur to get a wife for his son, Isaac. Eliezer obeys, travels to Ur, and stands outside Ur's city wall by a watering trough as women come refilling water jugs in the evening cool. First, Eliezer has obeyed to this point. Now he prays. Listen:

You, LORD, are the God my master Abraham worships. Please keep Your promise to him and let me find a wife for Isaac today. The young women of the city will soon come to this well for water, and I'll ask one of them for a drink. If she gives me a drink and then offers to get some water for my camels, I'll know she is the one You have chosen and that You have kept Your promise to my master.[164]

Get Practical. See the points in Eliezer's beautiful (answered) prayer. Eliezer —

- Is at ease with God.
- Converses with God.
- Is specific.
- Looks for a very specific answer.
- Prays *in motion* he already faithfully follows as he prays.

---

[164] Genesis 24:12-14.

Living in Sovereignty While Here on Earth

See how else prayer connects us to our God in these verses. You might want to cut these out and put them on your mirror in the bathroom.

Prayer brings God's power into your life:

> Summon your power, O God; show us Your strength, as You have before.[165]

> You are the God, Who performs miracles. You display Your power among the nations.[166]

Prayer puts God's power at your disposal:

> Counsel and sound judgment are mine; I have understanding and power.[167]

> The weapons we fight with are not the world's weapons. No, ours have divine power to demolish strongholds.[168]

> God did not give us a spirit of timidity, but a spirit of power, of love and of self-discipline.[169]

Prayer takes you beyond "power" as well:

> [God says]: "Not by might nor by power, but by my Spirit."[170]

> [Jesus] "My grace is sufficient for you, for My power is made perfect in weakness."[171]

> [Paul] He may strengthen you with power through His Spirit in your inner being.[172]

---

[165] Psalm 68:28.

[166] Psalm 77:14.

[167] Proverbs 8:14.

[168] 2 Corinthians 10:4.

[169] 2 Timothy 1:7.

[170] Zech. 4:6.

[171] Cor. 12:9.

[172] Ephes. 3:16.

I want you to see Me

Prayer allows us to know God:

The Lord spoke to Moses face to face, as a man speaks with his friend.[173]

Prayer shows us God's Compassion:

Your compassion is great, O LORD.[174]

Jesus . . . said, "I have compassion for these people."[175]

Prayer builds God's character in you, perfects you:

But the fruit of the Spirit is love, joy, peace, patience, kindness, goodness, faithfulness, gentleness and self-control.[176]

In prayer, we learn boldness:

"[The early Christians prayed] "Now, Lord, consider their threats and enable your servants to speak Your Word with great boldness." *After they prayed, the place where they were meeting was shaken. And they were all filled with the Holy Spirit and spoke the word of God boldly.*[177]

Prayer takes us to the far reaches of God's sovereign plan:

I promise that when any two of you on earth agree about something you are praying for, my Father in heaven will do it for you. Whenever two or three of you come together in My name, I am there with you.[178]

So God ordained ways for us to pierce through being earthbound to know Him.

- He gives us obedience so that we can pass through and graduate from His labs where He completes us.

---

[173] Exodus 33:11.

[174] Psalm 119:156.

[175] Matthew 15:32.

[176] Galatians 5:2223.

[177] Acts 4:29, 31.

[178] Matthew 18:19.

Living in Sovereignty While Here on Earth

- He gives us prayer so we can know His power, and see His leading, see Him ordering our steps.

- If it takes faith to see Him order our steps, then He has even ordained that the required faith completes us, grows us, and perfects us! God's provision awaits you. Now, you will — ?

Whether we tiptoe in surf watching a warm sunset or brace ourselves in a merciless storm; we trust, we worship to be stretched, and we confidently or desperately pray to God who loves us so much. Those times of trust and prayers help us live out our love back to our sovereign God while earthbound.

Trusting God's sovereignty will not determine whether or not you're saved, but it makes all the difference in the trip. All the difference.

9

The Lord is Willing

*Hamlet never argued with Shakespeare
for more lines or a kinder regard.*

*Tolkien wrote of a man better at painting exquisite,
painstaking leaves rather than trees. He hoped to illustrate
a bigger masterpiece, but the time he might devote to it he
selflessly gave to people in need. On entering Heaven,
he was wonderstruck to see the whole tree of which
his vision of perfect leaves had been a part.*[179]

Is it easier for those living in eternity, who live in heaven? They see God in all His glory, Lord of all, Master of every created thing and know He is sovereign. It is often not so easy to see Him here.

Earthbound, on this side of death we endure war, catastrophe, and people blaring on bullhorns that God is dead; or He's at fault; or we're all we have or our fates are in our hands.

So, how can we know God's will down here, earthbound?

Gary: One evening, I was talking to a friend who said, "If God is willing, I will be at the men's study tomorrow evening." I responded half-jokingly, "The Lord *is* willing." I then wondered, "Is saying that

---

[179] Tolkien. J. R. R. (1945). *Leaf by Niggle* in *The Dublin Review*.

I want you to see Me

actually consistent with my belief about God?" Good question. My friend was safe in what he said in light of this passage:

> *"Now listen, you who say, 'Today or tomorrow we will go to this or that city, spend a year there, carry on business and make money.' Why, you do not even know what will happen tomorrow. What is your life? You are a mist that appears for a little while and then vanishes. Instead, you ought to say, 'If it is the Lord's will, we will live and do this or that.' As it is, you boast in your arrogant schemes. All such boasting is evil."*[180]

My friend knew, that a first step to living in God's sovereignty is acknowledging Him as directing our lives: "If it is the Lord's will." His rule enters our days — not in a formula, but in how we live. We say and live as if the *Lord wills* is bedrock, it is first in living. Our conversations and resulting actions point to His sovereignty.

We don't usually write like this, but we need to write in an analytical, systematic way. Stay with us. When Gary's friend said, "If God is willing" his friend was possibly kidding — but still right — whether he knew it or not. For his friend to be right, we must answer a couple of questions.

1. Can we be certain in some things that "The Lord is *always* willing?"

2. What might it mean that "The Lord is willing" on a given issue?

The Lord gave commandments to show how He sees everything. Let's start here as our most certain points of "the Lord is willing." His first commandment is to worship the Lord. He reinforces it by forbidding idols in the second one.[181]

---

[180] James 4:13ff.

[181] Exodus 20:23.

The Lord is Willing

How God gave extravagantly of Himself to be in relationship with us! He desires to be our God. Our prodigal God[182] gives exuberantly. He spends lavishly in His love for us.

The Bible repeatedly warns us not to put other gods between us and God. And yet.

And yet, God healed Naaman[183] of leprosy. He wholeheartedly believed in Elisha's sovereign God of miracle. He packed bags of Elisha's dirt so when he worshipped God back in Aramea, he would bow down on Israel dirt to worship God purely. But he questioned Elisha about a yearly duty.[184] Once a year Naaman's king leaned on him to walk into Rimmon's Temple (think State Religion of Israel's arch enemy) to worship. Could he enter the temple with his king — and bow?

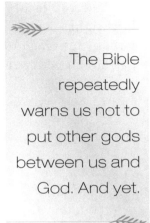

> The Bible repeatedly warns us not to put other gods between us and God. And yet.

Elisha: "No problem!"[185]

God *excluded* the first two commandments for that man.

Think of it: God exempted Naaman once a year from the first two commandments! It was God's will for this new believer to return home and live for God, even in a yearly trip into Rimmon's temple! Naaman's life worked — by God's sovereign design — but not as a result of formulas.

Consider another commandment to see if it is *always* God's will. God commands us to honor mother and father. The first commandment with a promise is also accompanied by a death sentence for failure.[186] And yet.

---

[182] T. Keller. (2009). *The Prodigal God*. Our thanks to Timothy Keller and his great book.
[183] Namaan commanded the army of Israel's arch enemy.
[184] 2 Kings 5:18.
[185] 2 Kings 5:19.
[186] Exodus 20:12.

I want you to see Me

And yet Jacob lied to his father, Isaac, to steal his brother's birthright — nullifying his father's authority. Jacob dishonored his father! Yet *that theft* formed the base for Jacob to become Israel's patriarch over twelve tribes.

God isn't limited to formulas.

God *excluded* the commandment, moreover: God used the exclusion to form His nation. Nowhere do we find Jacob repentant about dishonoring his father, Isaac.

God can exclude. Moreover He can use the exclusion. God is not limited to formulas.

So even in the commandments, God is not 100 percent predictable on "You can always know God wills THIS." God is higher than the laws He gave; He makes *exclusions* to laws He gave. Above the laws He gave, He can make exclusions we can't comprehend. God uses exclusions to His glory.

So if you are hunting formulas, put this book back, and go find someone handing out formulas. They can't always work because God is bigger than formulas. If they always worked, we could substitute surefire formulas for faith in Sovereign God. No formula is always true, but you may feel better — until God shows you formulas don't bind Him. He makes laws to use as needed. Only God saves. Only God gives hope, not formulas.

See two problems with formulas. One, some people settle for them, which is why cults flourish. Cults *seem to* answer all questions, have a formula for every need. They seemingly tame God, and make man (cult leaders) look strong and in control.

Second, detractors point to when formulas fail to say religion and god fail. Worse, they point out people following formulas to crazy extremes, to show how crazy religion is.

Formulas hinder us proclaiming how wild it is to follow a sovereign God! So back to Gary's statement, are there choices where we can say, "God *is* willing?" Yes.

The Lord is Willing

Two people wed before friends and family. God wants them to succeed and says, "I **hate** divorce."[187] He **is** willing. Does God want us to gather with others and invent ways to encourage each other? Absolutely![188] He **is** willing! If you profess Christ, God wills that you persist in Christ, flourish in loving God — one of our two key verses is the heart of this: "And I am certain of this: that He who began a good work in you is faithful, and He will complete it in the day of Christ."[189]

If you can fulfill a scriptural command or promise, God **is** willing. God placed His Holy Spirit's power in you — all you need to complete a promise.

So does God put power and resources at our disposal that we don't use to keep promises? Yes! **How often**? Ask it another way. How many people do you know using *all* His resources in faithful obedience? Subtract them from the rest of the Body of Christ. So many Christians do not option all God has for us.

Did God see that? Of course. Will He then use our disobedience to glorify Himself? Absolutely. Can He use our disobedience and selfishness for our good? Don't you just hope so? Well, know so. Now a warning: would you **really, willingly choose** to be a test case to disobey God — so He uses your disobedience for your good anyway? Paul asked and answered it this way: "What should we say? Should we keep on sinning, so that God's gift of undeserved grace will show up even better? **No**!" (*Never! No Way!*)[190]

No believer in her right mind ever wants to be that person, even though a sovereign God promises to use even our disobedience to our good.[191] The Lord **is** willing! Is that the same for us all? No.

---

[187] That stings when we write it. Malachi 2:16.

[188] Hebrews 10:25.

[189] Philippians 1:6-8.

[190] Romans 6:12.

[191] Romans 8:28.

I want you to see Me

Follow what you trust is His will. Watch cautiously if He uses an exclusion to His glory once in a great while.

So, how many *players* must I consider as I live in sovereignty? How many people figure into God's will for my life? Theologians and philosophers start with something called *agency*. Who can act on his or her own, fully, responsibly?

Agency

As you consider "agency" in the universe, you find that the Bible develops its answer over time. First, what is "agency?"

Agencies, plural

1 Action or intervention, esp. such as to produce a particular effect
— a belief in various forms of supernatural **agency**
2 A thing or person that acts to produce a particular result
— the movies could be an **agency** molding the public's values.

Web definitions

— Agency is a philosophical concept referring to an agent's capacity to act in a world.[192] — In the social sciences, agency refers to individuals' ability to act independently; to make their own free choices.[193]

The Bible starts simply talking about agency — it talks about one: God. God is a complete list of agents as the opening book begins: "In beginning, God created" everything.[194]

God created Adam and Eve to place in a garden called Eden. Even as we believe they were actual people, who lived as we do, their names also imply that their story is our story. Adam's name means *mankind*. Eve's name means *mom*.

---

[192] en.wikipedia.org/wiki/Agency_(philosophy).

[193] en.wikipedia.org/wiki/Agency_(sociology).

[194] Genesis 1:1 ff.

The Lord is Willing

The Garden story explodes as a serpent pushes Eve to question if God told her the whole truth about the garden.[195] The serpent isn't in a list of created stuff for Eden. Hm. Created before Eden? So one question is, was Satan (the Serpent) an agent, completely free and original in His actions?

The Bible answers this big question in sovereignty in another book, Job. As Job opens, we see creatures God created before Eden:

One day the angels came to present themselves before the Lord, and Satan also came with them. The Lord said to Satan, "Where have you come from?"

Satan answered the Lord, "From roaming throughout the earth, going back and forth on it."

Then the Lord said to Satan, "Have you considered my servant Job? There is no one on earth like him; he is blameless and upright, a man who fears God and shuns evil."[196]

Satan is on par with angels: all of them evidently created before Eden. See also: ***God begins*** the Job discussion, not Satan. In fact, as Job's story continues, Satan must get God's permission to touch Job's life. It shows Satan created for God's sovereign purpose. Satan is an agent, but not a free agent. He is under God's sovereign control like Job. Job endured nothing from any surprise agency — geology, bacteria, viruses or governments. Job acknowledged: it was all from God.

What happened to Job came at Satan's hand, but *only* in God's express permission. Satan's agency is in God's hands. Period. Like gravity, this is true independent of our feelings, beliefs, or wishes.

Further, God made Adam, Eve and Job to be agents as well. They think. They feel. They decide and believe. Most importantly,

---

[195] Genesis 2:1ff.

[196] Job 1:6-8.

I want you to see Me

they act. And they live and die and pass on their faith in God. Do you personally know all of the agents in your life? No, because our elected officials are agents in our lives, and further, God put them there, and we are responsible as God's children to pray for them.[197]

You have many other agents in your life: parents, siblings, and extended family; your neighbors and business associates; your doctors, dentist and lawyer; your pastor, counselor, and other helpers: and then there is the news. Watching the Twin Towers fall had a profound effect on all who watched them tumble.

That is a lot of agents. Hundreds, thousands of unpredictable people flesh out my agents map in my life. People spend years in therapy sorting the effects of agents on them.

Is the picture getting a little complex for you? Me, too. But increasing complexity drives all we know. See another example: the solar system.

Tom: growing up I memorized a solar system model where planets circled in neat orbits around our sun holding them in its gravity, as our moon was held by earth's gravity. Neat. Clean. Oh, add asteroids. Then some comets. Simple enough. Gravity held it all together working predictably. We figured it out. We were proud.

But Mercury scooted a little faster each year.[198] And we discovered the Kuiper Belt holding more planetoids Pluto's size, and now the Oort Belt. Is that complex enough, yet? Then add these.

Using the gravitational pull of hundreds of thousands of objects (asteroids, comets, plutinos, centaurs, planetary fragments, and debris) scientists now have a more realistic image of planetary and moon orbits. But it takes a supercomputer modeling the gravity fields of hundreds of thousands of agents to predict the planets' orbits and it took supercomputers modeling all those objects'

---

[197] Romans 13:12.

[198] An observable proof in one of Einstein's four papers in 1905.

The Lord is Willing

gravity on each other to explain irregularities in the orbits of Neptune, Pluto, Uranus — and even the giant Saturn — which they now theorize leapt orbits inside Neptune and Uranus!

All this is our solar system! It is complex beyond imagining!

Let the complexity humble you. Just using *gravity* (no free choice!) from objects in our solar system to explain the planets' orbits has taken thousands of years and continual revisions in theory and now supercomputers — and we still see gaps in our knowledge. We *all* live by faith.

We can't explain something as simple as planetary orbits as we don't know all the objects comprising our solar system, their formation(s), and their gravitational effect on each other over time.[199]

Increasing complexity — and that accounts only for gravity. Planets have no free choice!

Again, the complexity humbles us. Only God who created them accounts for them and projects their orbital futures so that *our* fragile Earth orbits in a hair's breadth of comfort for life. And.

On the other end of science, a host of subatomic particles now populate an atom's universe. And our bodies hold thousands of organisms enabling or interfering with every aspect of our health. The more we know, the more complexity explodes explanations and multiplies questions dancing beyond our answers!

Want you to go home, draw the curtains, and retreat? How to begin to sift through it all to make sense of this life God gives us?

It is too much. Take a breath. Zoom out. Start with some realities. Realities work no matter how complex the universe gets.

---

[199] These are visible parts of a solar system. We're still missing 93 percent of the mass of the system according to leading astrophysicists.

I want you to see Me

Realities

God made it.

The Bible starts as He creates all of it and ends with Him closing shop.

Start with sin: God did.

Sin entered our picture in the Garden of Eden. In Gary's book, *Thank God They Ate the Apple!* we posit that God has us in Plan A. Plan A casts us as sinners. We all work in that vantage point. No other option is working in our world.[200] No other operating system is available for a human computer. In fact, the Bible's first chapters say two things. One, God did it and He is not hiring defenders for His work: and two, sin is part of the given.

In our world choosing is neutral. We continually choose — God's will or rebellion (sin), but whether each choice is good or bad remains in God's hands *as* we follow Christ.[201] God uses our bad as well as our good choices to complete us and perfect us in His power. Notice it is God, Who is perfect in power, not us in choosing! Thank God He uses it all for our good.

Add death.

Death **came in with** sin. In the Bible, death shortened our life expectancy from hundreds of years down to 72.[202] Death follows sin everywhere sin goes.

---

[200] With great deference to CS Lewis and the *Space Trilogy*, and other Christian authors who have imagined what a world would look like where Adam and Eve never chose against God, we still live in a world where Adam and Eve sinned and so do we all.

[201] Nowhere do we say that everyone has this promise. Only Christians possess this promise.

[202] Genesis Chapter 4 gives the ages of the first people ranging up past eight and nine hundred years. After the flood in Chapter 5, those ages fall to what we expect today.

The Lord is Willing

Add separation.

Separation from God came with sin. David eloquently tells our side of this wasting pain in Psalms 32 and 51. David withered under sin's killing burden, agonizing over God's seeming absence in the wake of his sin in killing a trusted comrade to get his wife.

Now add Impossible Restoration.

As early as Adam's two sons, Cane and Abel, God effected an offering to restore our relationship with Him. God chose a blood sacrifice (like Abel's) to atone for (pay for) sins. The animal sacrifice system was repetitive. God's followers repeatedly sacrificed unending numbers of animals to restore their relationships to God. They sacrificed repeatedly to —

Get to "Zero." Wishing we could grow past it.

They spent all their religious energy getting to "zero" with God — forgiven up to this moment in my life — to begin again with God, only to fail and need another sacrifice to begin again, and begin again, and again. Animal sacrifices restored us to begin again: at zero with God. Endlessly repeating those sacrifices created a need, our greatest need. We needed —

For God to give a one-time sacrifice.

Only a onetime sacrifice enables our escape from continually spending our energy in cycles to get to zero with God — forgiven up to this moment. Only with this, can we be forgiven for all sins — past, present and future — so we can begin and build something new in our lives; sure of our relationship with God the Father.

Jesus Christ came.

He came as God's perfect sacrifice, a perfect Lamb — perfect to God. Impossibly, Jesus also came as our High Priest who was given a seat next to God. It is called the Mercy Seat. Jesus is God's mercy

I want you to see Me

representative on your behalf. He is God, Man, Lamb, and High Priest — everything rolled into ONE perfect, therefore once-for-all sacrifice.

- Jesus brought new life.
- So we now grow in Christ rather than start over after every, every sin. We don't have to get saved every time we go to church.
- So now God spends time perfecting and completing us.
- **All that means** Philippians 1:68 and Romans 8:28 work in God's plan for us as God's elect![203]

We can *join in with God* as Abraham did in faith to be on an obedience track of fellowship.[204] Jews celebrate this as wisdom,[205] and then as righteousness by faith.[206] Chris built on righteous by faith.[207] God counts our faith as righteousness.

What will you do?

God hands everything good to Christians. As part of His elect, as one He chose, you are forgiven to be in a love relationship with God.

God knows our choices

So how does life come from sovereign God to us: the earth-bound? Life comes as *choices*. That God knows an outcome of our choice does not render choosing any less important. That God knows an outcome does not lessen its impact. That God knows our

---

[203] This is God's name for us, His chosen ones who enjoy a saving fellowship with Him.

[204] This is the point of Abraham's story in Galatians, in Romans, and in *Experiencing God* by Henry Blackaby.

[205] Wisdom is celebrated in Proverbs, Ecclesiastes and some of the Psalms.

[206] Habakkuk 2:4.

[207] Romans 1:16-17 as it quotes Habakkuk 2:4.

The Lord is Willing

choices does not make any choice any easier. Consider a lesson from history.

On December 31, 1862 Abraham Lincoln walked the White House halls all night. In deep anxiety and prayer; and assailed by many troubling thoughts he weighed whether to sign the Emancipation Proclamation the following morning.

No less than our future hung in the balance.

Many *hoped* he would sign it: abolitionists, slaves, freedmen, and millions who saw a horrific war caused by this sin of owning another person. Many *feared* he would sign it: the South, southern sympathizers, and those who saw no way to restore the Union with no slaves for the South's economy. In DC a few people *knew* he would sign it.

But for all everyone hoped, feared or knew; Lincoln still wrestled all night — alone. The Emancipation Proclamation holds no less importance because God knew he would sign it. It held no less drama and it worked in the lives of all concerned no less. God still knew, as God had ordained for Abe to sign. Abe still reached for a pen and dipped it in the ink well freely as God had worked in his young heart from the first slaves he saw treated meanly on an Ohio riverboat on which he was catching a ride.

God knew, and it did not lessen the adventure, the anxiety or sheer suspense for everyone.

You may have already thought of this. Lanna and Gary were watching Jack Bauer save the world on the TV series *24*. They raptly watched Jack fight to preserve the United States, face down our worst enemies, and strive to do all it took to bring down bad guys.

Gary's not the get-two-hankies before a movie (Tom is) because we get sucked in. But he caught himself tightly holding the arm of his chair with his gut tightening as he worried about Jack!

173

I want you to see Me

Gary: after a while it hit me (smart man that I am, I did not interrupt Lanna's thrill of watching and cheering for Jack.) It hit me that the script was completely written, discussed, and rewritten. The show was cast, rehearsed, scenes built and wardrobes assembled. It was filmed, filmed with alternate endings, the dailies were screened, and the show moved through post production so Lanna and I could watch along with millions of others — this finished outcome!

The completed script now sat on a hundred desks and in garbage cans. It would not change, no matter how much Lanna or I wanted to see one character spared, or that one dispatched! It was beyond changing, but how thrilling it was to enjoy it! With each turn of that *unchangeable* script, we were scared, excited, hopeful, and anxious as our hearts raced.

For every movie, every show: we cheer, weep, smile, and hope for characters whose fates were written and unalterably produced before our viewing enjoyment — with no power of being an editor extended to us!

Cannot God's will and scripting our lives be at least as amazing and adventurous, as wild and unpredictable as Jack and the *24* writing team?

Seeing our choices in His sovereignty

God is sovereign over our choices.

God gave us all our needs, drives, hungers and desires. He also presents our choices. Does He influence our choosing? Absolutely.

Gary: I tell a story to help people grasp this. Standing in a kitchen, a ten-year-old boy excitedly told his friends he wanted a blue bicycle for Christmas!

Mom overhearing knew she and Dad already bought a red one that now waited in Grandma's garage! She and Dad went to work, and what color bike did the boy want by Christmas? Red. His

The Lord is Willing

parents used every picture, every ad, every bike peddling by, and not a few stories to influence their child so that on the day he was to receive his red bike, he wanted that very thing.

Tom: I have heard Gary tell that story a few times, and can only laugh at how true it is. In third grade the rage among my buddies were hefty Huffy bikes. All five friends with whom I rode bikes got one for birthdays: beefy bikes sporting painted steel and chrome. I still rode a little boy, first-grade bike.

My parents went to work, buying me a bike for Christmas and storing it. Unlike all my friends, mine was an English three speed with a gear shifter on the handle like a motorcycle! They showed me pictures of bicycle racers, talked about riding bikes long distances and pointed out three-speeds in Sears and at a bike shop.

Santa brought my sister a horse, my older brother a moped, and me a three speed, decidedly not heavy bike. Mom had done well. She only asked, "Want to take it around the block?" I needed permission to go so far on a bike!

So on a sunny, crisp Christmas day I rode out the driveway, into a mild wind and after adjusting the seat down, sped around the block: a hitherto long, distance. In third gear, I positively flew. I made it around the block far faster than I had ever ridden a bike!

On returning, my dad greeted me with **the** question: "Do you think any of your friends can keep up?" And they could not. Ever. I think I am the only one of us all still riding regularly. Do I think it was terrible; my parents influencing me toward a three speed? Not later today as I enjoy the wind in my hair.

Don't you think God's choices for us, His children, are the wisest, best avenues to perfect us?

God is sovereign over our sin

Placing our choices in God's sovereign will never makes a choice easier or some outcomes less frightening. God being sovereign even over our sin uses even our sin to perfect us. God exposes our sin. He uncovers it in His light for us to leave it behind. Even as God shows it to us, He presents us a choice. Paul says this is hard to grasp emotionally.[208]

Precisely here we began saying at the first of the book — we have much to unlearn, to begin learning all scripture teaches.

It may take you a while to get here: God is the only place to leave our sin. In the Bible, God's people matured through stages in understanding His sovereignty. In the same way that Adam and Eve lived, yet their story is our story, the same is true about how the Jews grew to grasp God as the only place to leave our sin. My individual story is reflected in the history of how the Jews grew to see God as sovereign, and the only place to leave our sin. Let's see some of their stages.

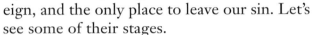

There are no other gods. Never were.

Early on the Jews believed something called henotheism: Our God is bigger than the gods of other countries. Or, my God's bigger than your god! Only a little before Christ did Ezra act in accord with true monotheism: There are no other gods. Never were. See this! About that same time true forgiveness finally hit home as Ezra prayed for God to forgive his sins, and all the sins of his country's history, so did Ezra see the only God as sovereign.

Odd. Think of it, monotheism and truly understanding forgiveness grew up in God's people together. As Jews grasped that God was one[209] and sovereign, they also grasped how God truly forgives us.[210] So for us — only when *we know* God is sovereign do *we know* that He forgives and uses even our forgiven sin to perfect us?

---

[208] Romans 7:13-19.

[209] The Shemah, at the core of Judaism says, "Hear oh Israel, the Lord our God is One!"

[210] Hebrews 8:12.

The Lord is Willing

Gary: consider Janet. We met as she had been in a therapy group at a treatment facility my client was suing. When asked if she witnessed my client being abused by the center she readily agreed. When I asked, "Will you testify on behalf of my client?" She said, "No!! I don't want to get involved!"

I left her alone for months. I was working on and praying over the case months later. I decided to call Janet again. The phone rang and she picked up.

We exchanged pleasantries and I asked again, "Have you reconsidered testifying on behalf of my client? It will truly strengthen her case."

First there was silence. Then quietly Janet asked, "If I testify, will they put me on trial, try to discredit me, embarrass me in front of a courtroom?"

I answered, "They will. It is how they do their job. They are not out to get you. They don't hate you. They are simply doing their job." She was quiet again. I held back.

Janet quietly said, "I'll testify. I actually was thinking about calling you."

I was surprised and asked, "Janet, may I ask what happened that caused you to change your mind about testifying?"

She responded, "Actually, I was raised Catholic, but my mother and I began attending Life.Church a few months ago and we were baptized recently. And God is working in my life! I knew I had to tell the truth about that center for Janet, but Mr. Richardson, I am petrified about what they will do when they cross-examine me. They know all the things I did when involved in drugs. They will use it all against me, to make me look bad, won't they?"

I stepped through the door she so fearfully opened. "Janet, do you believe God has a purpose for everything that happens in our lives?"

"Yes. I am coming to see that."

I want you to see Me

"Then, Janet, if God has heard you confess what you did when you were taking drugs, do you believe He has forgiven you?"

"Of course I believe that."

"Janet," I asked, "Do you see that as beautiful?"

Her silence gave way to quiet sobbing. "Yes. I think so."

"Janet, it is not until you believe a sovereign God truly and completely forgave you that you can face what happened, face what you did without shame, openly unafraid."

She regained her composure enough to ask, "How is that possible?"

I gently pushed her to see more: "Janet, when you have God's forgiveness, then there is nothing any lawyers doing their job can bring up that God has not forgiven, cleansed you from, and freed you from. True?"

With increasing firmness in her voice, she processed the statement. "That would be true. . . ."

I added, "That's who you were, but by God's wonderful grace, Janet, that's not who you are today."

So Janet began to prepare to face her greatest horror. Sitting in a room to take her deposition, someone would type a transcript as strangers — lawyers — unfolded her entire, sordid drug experience trying to leverage each revelation to discredit her as a witness for her friend.

Those lawyers had the wrong girl. Did they ever have the wrong girl! At her deposition Janet told her story, even surprising me. She told it all, dabbing her eyes to protect her mascara. She even told parts of her story she had left out when sharing with me: telling when she stole money and jewelry to buy drugs.

As the other lawyers probed further Janet threw them a curve ball making her an unshakable witness, and that you should keep in your bag of life truths.

The Lord is Willing

They asked dryly, "Are all of these allegations true?"

Janet quietly said, "Yes, but those are who I was. Not who I am!"

It caught the lawyers so much by surprise they asked her to repeat it, and she obliged, "All of those things are who I was. Not who I am!"

Janet saw a beauty in forgiveness by a God so big that He allows us to face our past and see His cleansing, healing hand so clearly that — it is all to His purpose and beautiful. Only then, did Janet come to aid her friend as an unshakable witness.

Do you see what Janet saw? "That's who I was. Not who I am!" Only a sovereign God gives such a gift!

> Beyond theory or theology; God's sovereignty gives us life.

Sin in Janet — in the form of drugs — ushered in death in her relationships and separation from all she loved. And yet, and yet God used all of it to bring her broken to Life.Church where God ushered her into new life beyond her death in drugs and her sin. God let all of her past die, so she could live free.

Beyond theory or theology; God's sovereignty gives us life.

I followed up with Janet and told her to focus on the beauty — to get her joy back. I smiled to quietly underscore a truth to Janet, "Sounds like a gift to me."

See it again. Until we can share shamelessly any darkness, share just how bad it was, we can't see healing's beauty. We can't fathom how God gives continual newness. Only a sovereign God heals us to say, "That is who I was. It is not who I am."

And see this in her story, only God, sovereign over our psychiatric makeup, emotional state, and our psycho-sexual state makes us forgiven and healed. Janet says, "That is who I was. It is not who I am." Can you?

I want you to see Me

Further, in Janet's life see that only Sovereign God can deliver us from bondage to our past and cultural past.[211] Whatever happened in her family, in her drug culture, in her parents' cultures — God freed her from them all. It takes a big God to set you free from all of it. It matters not if your culture was racist, judgmental, abusive or sin-drenched. God will set you free from that. He is that big. That loving.

He is that forgiving.

We find God's peace in admitting the sin in our past. Then we find He has made us a new person in Him. Until we can openly admit who we were before God set us free from it, it still holds us in bondage.

Gary: finally, please grasp one last fact from Janet. We can't know the truth of anyone else's experiences. So use restraint. Shy away from pronouncements and judgments. I might have judged her wrongly and tried to cajole her — only to drive her away from what God was doing. I took her no, kindly hung up and waited a few months. I did not try to fill in who *Janet* was with what I thought or what my experiences had taught me. I waited for God and Janet to fill in the-Janet-God-was-making.

Remember Jonah? Jonah, like some current-day preachers who beat up listeners, was thrilled to go in and sling theological bulls eyes as God's gunslinger, but he couldn't handle it when God called an entire city of people Jonah hated to repent and they did, and worse, God forgave them!

Serving Sovereign God and prejudging people are mutually exclusive. He is big, He can and will use you anyway, but prejudging will never put you in a place where you are most likely to be used of God. Worse, Jonah missed joy in God's miracle! At the end of his story, he's angrier over a vine eaten by a worm than excited about a million people God forgave!

---

[211] (Isaiah 49:5, Isaiah 42:5) and Nehemiah and Ezra's prayer.

The Lord is Willing

Humbly be prepared to be amazed by who God blesses, and who God uses — especially if it is you!

God uses Christians' obedience. If obedience was always Christians' response for all situations all the time, then this world would be profoundly different and this book would consist of one page and be unneeded.

AND God also uses people who do not follow Him. He used Pharaoh and Sennacherib's egos to show His children His deliverance and protection. He used a Persian king to bankroll rebuilding Jerusalem's walls.

AND, God uses people who follow Him and who fail Him (that's us).

AND like Jonah, God uses people who are rebelling against Him, and He even uses their rebellion to make them more complete. And in all of this, God says to you,

I want you to see Me.

If you didn't get this the first time through: read the book again. God gives us freedom to choose, unless what we choose conflicts with God's finishing us, completing us.

AUTHOR CONTACT

If you would like to contact the authors, find out more information, purchase books, or request them to speak, please contact:

GARY L. RICHARDSON
garyrichardsonspeaks.com

TOM WESTBROOK
beemersdad@aol.com

DAVID WILLETS
silverlining.ws

AUTHOR PRODUCT

Additional books, audio, and teaching from Gary Richardson
can be found at garyrichardsonspeaks.com.

Books

Fear Is Never Our Friend

Thank God They Ate the Apple!

Black Robe Fever

Audio

Fear is Never Your Friend

Teaching Set

Winning In The Courtroom